Storm at the Edge: A guide to DDoS Survival

Verses Kindler Publication

Verses Kindler Publication.

Website: www.verseskindlerpublication.com

Storm at the Edge: A guide to DDoS Survival

By: Mr. Pratik M. Lotia

ISBN: 978-93-49532-86-1

1st Edition

Price: INR 299/$15

Disclaimer

Storm at the Edge: A guide to DDoS Survival is authored by Pratik M. Lotia. The entirety of this published work comprises the original content of the author, who has undertaken diligent efforts in its editing. The characters depicted herein may be fictitious or inspired by real events; however, they are not intended to cause offense or represent any prejudice against any caste or system. Any similarity to the names of actual individuals, locations, or institutions is purely coincidental and serves the narrative. The author bears sole responsibility for the originality of this work; the publisher assumes no liability thereof.

"To my wife, who believed in me..."

"Security is the person, not the tool"

Acknowledgments

Writing a book about the ever-evolving landscape of DDoS and botnets has been a journey that required the support, expertise, and patience of many individuals. This work would not have been possible without the following people.

Professional and Technical Support

First and foremost, I would like to thank the technical reviewers who dedicated their time to ensuring the accuracy and depth of this book. Your insights into ISP backbone routing, scrubbing center architectures, and application-layer mitigation were invaluable.

I am particularly grateful to Rich Compton, my mentor, for the countless hours of whiteboarding and for teaching me the intricacies of DDoS. Your guidance in involving me in various working groups and projects was fundamental to my growth; it is from you that I truly learned the craft of DDoS defense. To my former manager Tyler Sutterby for providing me the freedom to explore, research and develop new projects. To my colleagues at Charter Communications, especially Charles Manser, Taylor Harris, Tom Bowlby, Avishek Gurung, thank you for the collaboration and the late-night incident responses that served as the primary classroom for this material.

Industry and Community

A special thanks to the broader cybersecurity community and the open-source contributors behind the tools mentioned throughout this book. Your commitment to a more resilient internet is the foundation upon which books like this are written.

I would also like to thank the team at Verses Kindler Publication; specifically my editor, Krish Chadha for seeing the potential in this project and guiding it from a rough outline to a finished volume. Your patience with technical jargon and shifting deadlines is deeply appreciated.

Personal Acknowledgments

On a personal note, I must thank my family.

To Priyanshi, thank you for being my rock while I was "lost in the weeds" of packet captures and protocol analysis. Your support during the long weekends and late nights spent writing was my greatest motivation.

To my parents, in-laws and sibling, thank you for reminding me to step away from the screen and for your curiosity about "what the bad bots are doing today."

Final Words

Finally, to the readers: thank you for your commitment to defending the digital frontier. This book is for you.

Pratik Lotia

About the Author - Pratik M. Lotia

Pratik is an accomplished infrastructure security engineer with over a decade of experience dedicated to safeguarding digital ecosystems. He focuses on building tools and processes for implementing security best practices for cloud native environments. He has extensive experience working on security projects for public & private clouds, and telecommunications security. He actively contributes to open-source security projects and has been a speaker at various conferences in the past.

Pratik oversaw important security projects at Charter Communications, one of the leading internet and wireless network service providers in America, before joining Reddit. His work focused on safeguarding cloud infrastructures, developing defences against high-impact threats such as botnets and DDoS attacks, implementing robust container security guardrails and sophisticated secret management practices, and designing scalable and cost-efficient, all-encompassing security solutions.

Pratik is involved with the Cloud Native Computing Foundation (CNCF) and is part of its Technical Advisory Group (TAG-Security), where he contributes to various projects. He served on the board of the Colorado chapter of Cloud Security Alliance for four years. Additionally, he is also a part of the alumni GOLD board at his alma mater, the University of Colorado Boulder, where he earned his Master's degree in Telecommunications. He is also an independent consultant, lending his expertise in cybersecurity to various organizations seeking specialized guidance and solutions. He holds a

Bachelor of Engineering in Electronics and Telecommunications Engineering from the University of Mumbai and is a certified GIAC Penetration Tester (GPEN).

Pratik holds seven U.S. patents related to DDoS mitigation and botnet mitigation. His past work has won him numerous accolades, such as being recognised in the top 50 innovators of India by Lockheed Martin in collaboration with the government of India, and being recognised as one of the top 25 entrepreneurs by the Tata Group. His thought leadership has been featured at prestigious conferences such as NANOG, KubeCon, BSides and Secure World.

Driven by the philosophy that "security is the person, not the tool," Pratik is deeply committed to educating individuals and fostering robust communities, all with the goal of securing our digital future.

Index

Storm at the Edge: A guide to DDoS Survival

In today's fast-paced digital world, businesses are rapidly adopting advanced technologies to stay competitive and enhance their services. However, this acceleration brings with it a growing wave of cyber threats. Among the most dangerous are Distributed Denial of Service (DDoS) attacks, which strike with alarming speed, precision, and unpredictability. Such incidents can inflict massive economic damage, tarnish a business's reputation, and severely disrupt critical operations. Often fueled by vast networks of compromised devices called botnets, these attacks represent a formidable challenge to digital resilience.

"Storm at the Edge" is your essential guide to navigating this complex security landscape. It provides an in-depth look at current cyber risks, with a particular focus on the intricate nature of DDoS attacks and the underlying threats posed by botnets. This book bridges the gap between technical understanding and strategic intent, offering practical strategies, realistic techniques, and tangible examples. We'll show you how to effectively integrate cybersecurity with broader business objectives, underscoring the crucial link between technological prowess and organizational success.

True digital transformation goes far beyond simply adopting new tech or migrating to the cloud. It demands a fundamental rethinking of how businesses operate and deliver value. To truly thrive, organizations must prioritize customer needs, foster innovation, break down silos, empower their teams, leverage analytics strategically, and cultivate synergistic collaboration across all departments.

This means security can't be an afterthought; it must be woven into every stage of a project's life cycle, from initial concept to final execution. Effective DDoS defense, alongside comprehensive protection measures, transcends the traditional IT domain—it becomes an organizational imperative. As cyber threats, including sophisticated botnet-driven attacks, continue to evolve in detail and intricacy, our defensive tactics must evolve right along with them

Who This Book Is For

This comprehensive guide is for anyone looking to understand and effectively combat DDoS threats, and the underlying botnet forces that often drive them. Whether you're a student embarking on an information security career, a system administrator tasked with protecting critical infrastructure, a business executive shaping strategic plans, or simply curious about the mechanics of the internet, this book is for you.

"Storm at the Edge" demystifies complex cybersecurity topics with clear explanations and well-structured insights. It offers actionable advice applicable across various roles and industries, providing readers with both the technical know-how and the strategic perspectives needed to succeed. No matter your goal—whether it's enhancing your technical readiness or strategically embedding security initiatives within corporate frameworks—this book will empower you to build resilience and foster cybersecurity-driven innovation.

Chapter 1: Introduction to Distributed Denial of Service (DDoS) Attacks

Understanding DDoS Attacks in Depth

One of the most disruptive weapons in the modern cyberthreat arsenal is probably a Distributed Denial of Service (DDoS) attack. DDoS attacks are loud, aggressive, and noticeable, as opposed with deliberate breaches intended to steal data or infiltrate systems covertly. Their sole objective is to overload a digital service such as an internet site, application, or network with so much traffic that it becomes unusable for its intended consumers.

In their simplest form, DDoS assaults use numerous individual systems, typically compromised devices, to direct a massive volume of requests or messages onto a targeted resource. These hacked systems result in a group of computers controlled by an attacker, referred to as a 'robot network' or more commonly, as a "botnet". Due to this network's dispersed architecture, DDoS attacks are extremely difficult to stop since malicious activity is obscured by traffic coming from a multitude of distinct IP addresses.

The intent is simple: drain the resources of the victim. This may entail consuming all the available bandwidth a network can provide, overloading a server's computing resources, or clogging application-layer resources such as APIs or login pages. Once the system is overwhelmed, it is unable to respond to rightful traffic, in effect denying service to its legitimate users or clients.

Even though Denial of Service (DoS) assaults have existed since the Internet's inception, for a long time, they only involved one or a small number of attackers. In the last twenty-five years, DDoS assaults have increasingly become more complex and of higher intensity, and are widespread nowadays. Attackers today have more options than ever to take advantage of their actions because of the growth of the Internet of Things (IoT), cloud computing, and always-on services.

The damage and service interruptions caused by a well-planned DDoS assault can be enormous in today's hyperconnected cyberspace. When such outages affect the vital infrastructure or services, organisations risk losing revenue, reputation, downtime, and even compliance penalties.

Goals and Objectives of DDoS

Fundamentally, a DDoS attack is an exercise in resource exhaustion. It's an attempt to overwhelm certain bounds of the system, be it CPU cycles, memory, bandwidth, or application-layer constraints, and drive those limits until the system slows down severely or crashes.

But the motivation behind a DDoS attack can range widely:

- Financial Loss: For e-commerce websites, streaming services, or service providers, even temporary downtime can translate into significant revenue loss. This renders them high-priority targets for financially driven attackers or as extortion targets.
- Damage to Reputation: Service outages can cause loss of customer confidence, adverse publicity in the press, and long-term reputational damage. In today's digital-first world

where users anticipate close-to-perfect uptime,a DDoS-triggered outage can have permanent repercussions.

- Competitive Sabotage: Sometimes competitor companies might engage in unethical practices by contracting saboteurs or operatives to interfere with a competitor's business during peak sales events or new product release periods.
- Ideological or Political Statement: Political or ideological hacktivist (activists who hack) groups usually employ DDoS attacks to make political or social statements. By targeting government websites or big corporations, they try to get attention for their cause.
- Diversion Tactic: More advanced attackers could employ DDoS as a diversion. As the IT and cybersecurity staff are occupied with mitigating the effects of the denial-of-service attack, a real threat like a stealthy data exfiltration or privilege escalation attempt, could be unfolding elsewhere The DDoS is merely a smokescreen to facilitate this espionage.
- Extortion/Ransom: This is a very common and direct financial motivation. Attackers launch a DDoS attack, or threaten to do so, and demand a ransom (often in cryptocurrency) to stop or prevent the attack. If the victim doesn't pay, they face continued disruption.
- Revenge/Personal Vendetta: Individuals or groups might launch a DDoS attack out of anger, resentment, or a desire for retaliation against a specific person, company, or organization they feel has wronged them. This can range from disgruntled former employees to individuals holding a grudge.

- "Fun" or Hooliganism/Testing Skills: Some attackers, often referred to as "script kiddies," engage in DDoS attacks simply for the thrill, to test their hacking skills, or to cause mischief without a clear, sophisticated motive beyond showing off or causing temporary disruption. They might target a school website, a gaming server, or any readily available target.
- Cyberwarfare/State-Sponsored Attacks: Nation-states can employ DDoS attacks as part of a larger cyberwarfare strategy. The goals here can be wide-ranging, including disrupting critical infrastructure (power grids, financial systems, telecommunications), interfering with communications, or causing widespread chaos to gain a strategic advantage.
- Competitive Intelligence (beyond simple sabotage): While competitive sabotage focuses on directly harming a competitor, some DDoS attacks might be designed to gather intelligence. For example, by causing a system to go offline, attackers might learn about a competitor's IT infrastructure weaknesses or response procedures.
- Testing Security Defenses: In some rare cases, a DDoS attack might be conducted by a white-hat hacker or security researcher (with permission, ideally) to test the resilience of a system's defenses. However, this is distinct from malicious intent.

Throughout all these situations, the common end is disruption. For financial motives, political messages, or strategic diversion, DDoS attacks are meant to create confusion, stress infrastructure, and challenge the resilience of an organization's cyber defenses. Consequently, detecting the attacker's intent is important in designing both technical countermeasures and general incident response.

DDoS vs. Other Cyber Threats

In the expansive world of cybersecurity, threats are numerous, there's ransomware, phishing, data breach, insider attack, and so many others. Each threat has its own risks, but DDoS attacks are different because they are so non-intrusive yet so disruptive. Unlike most cyber threats, whose purpose is to access, steal, or corrupt data, DDoS attacks are essentially about denial of access.

The basic distinction is in intent and effect. A data breach, for example, is an unauthorized access to confidential information, credit card numbers, personal data, business secrets, usually resulting in regulatory actions and financial loss. Ransomware locks files, requiring payment for release. Phishing tricks users into surrendering credentials. These attacks are stealthy, aimed, and frequently necessitate extensive post-incident restoration.

DDoS attacks, on the other hand, are public, instant, and noisy. They don't use stealth or deception. Rather, they try to bring services down by inundating them. There is no theft of data involved, but the consequences nonetheless can be dire. A large DDoS attack can result in system downtime, customer frustration, SLA breaches, and even affect stock prices for publicly traded entities.

There also exists a difference in how defenses are organized. Conventional cyber-attacks are usually addressed by endpoint security, firewalls, intrusion detection systems, and anti-malware software. These depend greatly on signature-based matching, behavior monitoring, and user education. DDoS defense, though, needs to have strong network-layer protection or application layer protection real-time traffic monitoring, and scalable infrastructure that can absorb huge amounts of illegitimate traffic.

Current Trends in DDoS Attacks

DDoS attacks have undergone radical changes in the last decade. What was once considered a nuisance reserved for smaller websites or gaming servers has become a tactical tool used against enterprises, governments, and critical infrastructure.

1. Larger Scale and Higher Frequency

Modern DDoS attacks are much more massive than those a few years ago. Multi-terabit-per-second attacks are no longer unusual. Clouds and large platforms have regular attacks exceeding the 1 Tbps barrier. These volumetric storms have never-ending power to overwhelm even fortified infrastructure. Moreover, the rate of attacks has risen, what was a rare occurrence is now a daily experience for most organizations.

2. Rise of Multi-Vector Attacks

Today's DDoS attacks are not constrained to any one type of traffic flood. Attackers now layer a variety of vectors into an individual campaign, i.e., blending TCP SYN floods, DNS amplification, and HTTP request floods all at once. It is much more difficult to mitigate multi-vector attacks since the defenders have to contend with layers of complexity all at the same time.

3. DDoS-as-a-Service Platforms

One worrying trend is the commercialization of DDoS attacks. On the dark web, "booter" or "stresser" sites provide DDoS-for-hire for a mere $10. These sites are not technically demanding and have simple user interfaces that enable anyone to easily carry out an attack. This has spawned a wave of opportunistic and revenge attacks, even by novice hackers.

4. Abuse of IoT Devices

Massive botnets have been built thanks to the sheer amount of Internet of Things (IoT) devices, many of which have inadequate default protection. Devastating IoT-powered attacks were demonstrated in 2016 by the infamous Mirai botnet, which brought down major DNS provider Dyn. New versions are constantly appearing that compromise everything from smart doorbells to routers.

5. Application-Layer Attacks Are on the Rise

Whilst volumetric attacks lead the headlines, there has been a developing movement in the direction of quieter, low-bandwidth application-layer DDoS attacks. They target depleting application resources instead of bandwidth, so they are more difficult to discover through standard monitoring tools. Attack types such as HTTP floods or Slowloris are also used more frequently to silently take down services.

6. Adaptive and Evasive Techniques

Today's attackers are evasive. They observe real-time defensive reactions and change their tactics during an attack. Some employ encrypted traffic to evade inspection tools, while others replicate legitimate user behavior to blend in. These new techniques emphasize the necessity of intelligent, behavior-based detection systems.

7. Short, Burst Attacks ("Hit and Run")

While large-scale attacks are still common, there's also a trend of shorter, high-intensity bursts designed to quickly overwhelm defenses and then disappear before effective mitigation can be fully deployed. These can be particularly disruptive for organizations that rely on manual intervention.

8. Horizontal/Carpet Bombing Attacks

Instead of focusing on a single IP address or server, attackers are increasingly distributing traffic across a wide range of IP addresses within a target's network. This makes it harder for defenses to detect and block, as the traffic volume per IP might remain below alert thresholds.

Types of DDoS Attacks

DDoS attacks may all aim to disrupt service availability, but they do so through different vectors and techniques. Broadly, these attacks fall into three categories: volumetric, protocol, and application-layer attacks.

1. Volumetric Attacks

Volumetric attacks seek to fill the provided bandwidth of a system, flooding network pipes with enormous traffic. They are the most prevalent types of DDoS and frequently include amplification methods to increase the traffic volume.

DNS Amplification: An open resolver is spoofed with a DNS query, and the open resolver sends back a much greater response to the victim, inundating them with information they never asked for.

NTP Amplification: Analogous in technique to DNS amplification, but it exploits the Network Time Protocol to produce high-volume responses.

Volumetric attacks are typically of large volume and can easily drown even powerful infrastructure if not dealt with quickly.

2. Protocol Attacks

Protocol attacks exploit vulnerabilities in Layers 3 and 4 of the OSI model, attempting to drain server resources or intermediate systems such as firewalls and load balancers.

- SYN Floods: The attacker floods with TCP/SYN packets to create handshakes, but never finishes them, thereby filling the connection table of the server.
- Ping of Death: Maliciously crafted pings that are larger than the packet size supported by the system result in buffer overflows and crashes.
- Smurf Attacks: The attacker sends ICMP with a spoofed source IP (the victim's), which results in several replies overwhelming the target.

Such attacks tend to look stealthy in terms of the volume of traffic but are very effective in bringing down services as well as impairing network devices.

3. Application-Layer Attacks

Attacking Layer 7, these attacks simulate legitimate user behavior in order to take advantage of application-specific functions and thus make them more difficult to detect.

- HTTP Floods: The attack involves sending ostensibly legitimate HTTP GET or POST requests at high velocities, using server resources and database connections.
- Slowloris: It initiates a large number of connections to the server and maintains them as long as possible by sending incomplete requests, thus occupying the server's connection pool.
- SQL Floods: Malicious database queries are repeatedly employed to overwhelm backend systems.

Application-layer assaults are particularly perilous in that they can bypass customary DDoS countermeasures and need to be detected by smart behavioral observation.

Real-World Case Studies

DDoS attacks are not an abstraction; it has brought down some of the world's largest and most protected networks. These actual case studies show the varied motives, methods, and consequences of massive DDoS attacks.

1. The Mirai Botnet Attack (2016)

When the Mirai botnet launched an unprecedented attack on Dyn, a well-known DNS service provider, in October 2016, it was one of the biggest DDoS attacks in history. Mirai generated a traffic flow exceeding 1 Tbps by compromising a multitude of Internet of Things devices, including recording devices, DVRs, and modems. In

North America and Europe, it led to disruption of services such asTwitter, Netflix, Reddit, and PayPal.

2. GitHub Attack (2018)

GitHub, the largest global code repository, was hit by a record 1.35 Tbps DDoS attack in 2018. It lasted approximately 20 minutes but was historic for employing a novel vector, memcached reflection that multiplied attack traffic by as much as 50,000 times. Attackers used misconfigured memcached servers to reflect enormous traffic to GitHub.

GitHub's implementation of an automated DDoS protection service enabled it to bounce back fast, and it set the standard for best-of-breed incident handling.

Understanding Botnets

At the core of the majority of contemporary DDoS attacks is a botnet, an army of compromised machines operated by one attacker or group. These machines, sometimes referred to as "zombies," are infected through viruses or attacked through unpatched vulnerabilities, then remotely orchestrated to cause massive attacks, unaware to the owner.

Botnets not only drive volumetric DDoS attacks but also have the ability to switch tactics during an attack, adjust defenses, and even send application-layer floods. Their versatility and scalability make them the backbone of contemporary cybercrime and a seemingly insurmountable challenge for defender's intent on ensuring service availability and trust.

Chapter 2: The Anatomy of a Botnet

Define Botnets and Their Lifecycle (Infection, Command and Control, Attack Execution)

A "botnet," which stands for "robot network," is a collection of internet-connected devices that have been infected by a malicious software (also known as mal-ware) and are controlled remotely by a single entity on the internet. Such compromised devices, also known as zombies or bots are covertly taken over often without the owner's knowledge and programmed to do coordinated malevolent actions. A powerful tool in the toolbox of cybercriminals, botnets enable them to launch massive attacks, particularly Distributed Denial of Service attacks, with catastrophic results.

The lifecycle of a botnet goes through three main phases: infection, command and control (C2), and execution of attack.

1. Infection

The initial penetration of the machines marks the beginning of the botnet life cycle. By using techniques like phishing emails, weak credentials, brute force, supply chain attacks, drive-by downloads, malicious files, or OS and program vulnerabilities the attackers exploit security flaws. The malware silently installs itself after completing its execution, granting the hacker remote access to the compromised system. Designed for stealth, it keeps the computer running normally while silently joining the ever-growing botnet.

In modern botnets, the infection is not just limited to traditional devices such as computers and home gateway routers. The proliferation of Internet of Things devices, usually poorly defended, has opened up the attack surface exponentially. Cameras, routers, smart thermostats, and even refrigerators may be taken over and recruited into botnets.

2. Propagation & Growth (Self-Propagation)

- Worm-like Capabilities – The malware continuously scans internal and external networks for vulnerable hosts, then self-replicates onto any it finds.
- Leveraging Stolen Credentials – Compromised usernames, passwords, and keys are reused to log in and seed new systems.
- Peer-to-Peer (P2P) Infection – Infected devices can directly pass the malware to neighbouring machines, removing reliance on a central server.
- Exploiting Local Network Services
    - Scans for open ports such as Telnet, SSH, or RDP.
    - Targets misconfigurations or unpatched routers, printers, and IoT devices to gain a foothold.

3. Command and Control (C2)

Once they become infected, the affected devices report to a central framework, commonly called the command-and-control system. This is where the attacker provides commands, and controls the botnet. In accordance with the complexity of the botnet, communication with C2 servers might take place over peer-to-peer networks, HTTP(S), or protocols like IRC (Internet Relay Chat).

A botmaster is the person or group that owns and remotely controls a botnet. C2 is used by botmasters to set up attack parameters, distribute updates, or instruct bots to carry out particular operations. The majority of botnets use fast-flux DNS or domain generation algorithms techniques to constantly switch C2 locations in order to evade identification and removal, we'll unpack in a section later on.

4. Attack Execution

Once invoked, the botnet performs its desired action. Data theft, cryptocurrency mining, spam emailing, and DDoS attacks are a few examples. Hundreds or thousands of compromised devices simultaneously flood an intended server with traffic during a DDoS attack, exhausting its capacity and rendering it unavailable to regular users.

5. Persistence & Evasion

A sophisticated botnet incorporates itself extensively to evade eradication rather than just striking and disappearing. Malicious files, registry keys, and processes are concealed by kernel-level rootkits, making them invisible to administrators and antivirus software. In the meantime, the malware's code is continuously changing its underlying configuration to evade detection by signature-based scanners by using multiple layers of concealment and polymorphism. Certain bots have a built-in anti-analysis feature, which restricts their activities or shuts it down entirely if they detect a virtual machine, sandbox, or debugger. Some variations also use scheduled or event-triggered logic, which does not activate until a specific date, time interval, or an external signal is received. In a separate evasion section, we'll go into more detail about these covert methods, including contemporary kernel trickery and polymorphic packers.

Architectures of C2 Controllers (Centralized vs. Decentralized)

Botnet architecture is a description of the way compromised devices (bots) talk to their master (the botmaster) and other bots. Generally speaking, botnet structures exist in two styles: centralized and decentralized(peer-to-peer).

Centralized Architecture

In a centralized botnet, all affected machines talk to a single set of command-and-control servers or a hierarchical ensemble of a few server sets. This architecture is analogous to a client-server system, with bots playing the role of clients being instructed by a central system. IRC, DNS, UDP, HTTP, or custom TCP protocols are typically employed for keeping in touch.

Benefits for attackers:

- Easy to set up and administer.
- Easy to command and harvest data from bots.

Disadvantages:

- Single point of failure: If the C2 server is detected and eliminated by defenders, the entire botnet can be disabled.
- Higher detectability: Centralized traffic patterns are relatively easier to track and analyze.

Well-known examples of centralized botnets include Storm (early versions) and Citadel.

Decentralized Architecture

There is no central controller in decentralized or P2P botnets. Each bot is capable of being both a client and a server, forwarding commands from and to peers. Communication is dispersed over a mesh-like structure, which makes the botnet more robust and harder to take down.

Advantages:

- Redundancy and fault tolerance.
- No single point of failure.
- Harder to trace and close down.

Disadvantages:

- Relatively difficult to create and manage.
- Slower dissemination of commands compared to a centralized control scheme.

Examples of decentralized botnets are Gameover Zeus and Sality.

Hybrid Architecture

Multiple control mechanisms are combined in a hybrid botnet, which typically consists of a small number of central C2 servers supported by a peer-to-peer overlay that may take over in the event that the primary servers fail. Because each bot may rely on P2P routing in the event that defenders take down the primary servers, this tiered system offers invaders the ideal combination of both worlds: quick and easy updates via the central tier and robust resilience. This model is exemplified by Conficker, ZeroAccess, and subsequent Storm variants, which maintain a network layer for redundancy while using HTTP or IRC for routine operations. Complexity is the trade-off: hybrid botnets require larger code bases, cautious key management, and generate a variety of traffic patterns that, with the right analysis, might provide defenders with new targets to pursue.

Attackers in today's cyber warfare tend to use hybrid frameworks, generally beginning with centralized management and eventually moving towards P2P formations, to couple simplicity and redundancy, making them even more difficult to identify and detect.

Covert C2 Channels

Many modern botnets use obscure protocols or common services that security tools rarely examine to conceal their C2 communications. Detecting such botnet communications becomes a major challenge as blocking access to services such as Twitter, Telegram, Discord, GitHub, or Pastebin can interfere with legitimate business operations and user activity. Bots may poll these platforms over protocols such as HTTPS DNS, etc., to download instructions contained in seemingly benign tweets or code commits. Others rely on ICMP and NTP, put commands into TXT records, or use DNS tunnelling, hoping that such small data packets will blend in with legitimate network traffic and evade detection by security monitoring systems. The distinction between malware chatter and regular web traffic is further blurred by more sophisticated streams that retrieve seemingly normal pictures or files (such as PDFs) with encrypted commands hidden in their pixel values or metadata.

Methods of Botnet Creation and Propagation (Malware, Vulnerabilities, Social Engineering)

Botnets don't magically appear, they are carefully built by attackers through a mixture of malware distribution, vulnerability exploitation, and social engineering techniques. These methods enable cybercriminals to infect many systems and integrate them into their botnet infrastructure.

1. Malware Deployment

The most straightforward way to establish a botnet is through malware propagation, malicious code that takes over systems and provides the attacker with remote access. Such malware tends to be self-copying or stealthy in nature to evade discovery. Upon installation, it quietly hooks the device up to a command-and-control (C2) network, waiting for further instructions.

Malware families most commonly utilized in botnet building are Mirai, Zeus, and Necurs. Mirai achieved prominence by exploiting IoT devices with default credentials, infecting them en masse after discovering them online.

Attackers utilize various delivery methods for malware:

- Phishing emails containing malicious attachments or links.
- Drive-by downloads from infected websites.
- Trojan programs or imitation updates masquerading as legitimate software.

2. Exploiting Vulnerabilities

Most botnets spread by exploiting software, operating systems, firmware, and network services through known and zero-day vulnerabilities. This is an exceptionally effective attack against devices that are misconfigured, outdated, or not properly secured.

Some examples are:

- Unpatched internet of things (IoT) devices and routers with exposed admin panels.
- Remote code execution (RCE) through web application vulnerabilities.
- Buffer overflow attacks and exploitation of privilege escalation features.
- Weak credentials & brute-force entry points, like default passwords on IoT devices (Mirai).
- Exploiting unpatched systems (e.g., WannaCry, EternalBlue).

Sophisticated botnets employ automated scanners that scan the internet for vulnerable devices. Once found, they immediately infect them, and even patch the exploited vulnerability to prevent other attackers from gaining access.

3. Social Engineering

Human error remains the most common vulnerability. Social engineering techniques trick users into doing something that exposes their systems, like clicking on malicious URLs or putting credentials on imitation websites.

Examples are:

- Spear-phishing aimed at specific entities or organisations.
- Spam security notifications are compelling users to download malicious antivirus software.
- Impersonation attacks via email or social media.

4. Supply Chain Offences

By breaching software suppliers, servers that manage distribution of software updates, or libraries maintained by third parties, the attackers in this case contaminate the well-trusted upstream services, allowing malware to infect reliable software. Smaller yet widely used libraries on open-source package registries, which are not well-maintained, are attacked every month.

Examples include:

- Injecting malicious code into software updates.
- Tampering with software builds or open-source components to infect every downstream consumer.

The Bot Client

Thousands or even millions of identical malware "clients" that covertly infiltrate infected computers power a modern botnet. Every client follows a straightforward life-cycle loop, which consists of maintaining a network connection to C2 endpoints, listening for commands, carrying out the assigned task, and reporting the outcomes. Usually, an exploit, malicious attachment, or drive-by download sends a tiny dropper that starts the infection. After negotiating an encrypted channel, an integrated communication module iterates through backup domain lists or a domain-generation mechanism until it establishes communication with the botmaster. An execution engine, typically scriptable, is at the core of the malware. It decodes incoming commands and loads the appropriate functional plug-in when needed.

The bot can change into any position the botmaster wants once it's online. A DDoS module may unleash SYN, UDP, or HTTP floods against a target; and components that snoop on user credentials before they even get to the point of browser encryption. Other plug-ins take screenshots, steal files, or use the host as a proxy to conceal the attacker's real location. More sophisticated bots even reveal complete remote-access capabilities, which enable the herder to perform arbitrary instructions, interactively browse files, and delve further into the victim's network. Modern botnets are versatile, profitable, and infamously challenging to eliminate because of their plug-and-play architecture, robust connectivity, and persistence techniques.

These attack vectors are frequently combined to achieve higher infection rates. For example, a phishing email may contain a malware-bearing attachment that installs malware, which then uses system vulnerabilities to ensure persistence, and then communicates with a botnet C2 server.

Types of Devices Often Enlisted into Botnets (Computers, IoT Devices, Mobile Devices)

In an effort to boost their power and extend their reach, attackers attack a wide range of network-connected devices. Almost any system with network connectivity, weak security controls, or out-of-date software can end up as a botnet node. The most frequently recruited device types are personal computers, Internet of Things (IoT) devices, and mobile devices.

1. Personal Devices

Due to their extensive use and high number of unpatched systems, Windows PCs have historically been the most common targets for botnet infections. These systems are ideal for launching spam campaigns, DDoS attacks, or credential grabs since they offer a lot of processing power, internet access, and storage.

2. Internet of Things (IoT)

IoT gadgets are a category of botnet targets that is expanding rapidly. These consist of smart TVs, video recording devices, routers and switches, heating and cooling systems, printing equipment, along with baby monitors. Since they are usually configured with default factory credentials, insufficient security features, and restricted firmware update capabilities, hackers view them as easy targets. The Mirai botnet famously took use of these vulnerabilities to perform one of the largest DDoS attacks ever.

3. Mobile Devices

Botnets are increasingly attacking tablets and smartphones, particularly those running older Android versions. Malware that was downloaded from third-party app stores or phishing websites can infect devices, allowing botnet activity. Due to their increasing prevalence, mobile devices are a scalable and valuable tool for hackers.

Mechanisms of Command and Control

Bot herders use Command and Control (C2) servers to send commands, gather data, distribute malware updates, and manage attacks on thousands or even millions of infected machines. The power and subtlety of a botnet frequently depend on the design and maintenance of its C2 structure. Historically, C2 systems have developed in three principal forms:

1. IRC (Internet Relay Chat)

One of the first botnet C2 methods used IRC channels. Every infected machine (bot) would join a designated IRC server and channel, where it would listen for commands relayed by the botmaster.

Pros:

- Simple to set up and observe bots in real-time.
- It is very simple, text-based communication.

Cons:

- Easy to target with network monitoring software.
- Susceptible to takedowns if the IRC server gets shut down or confiscated.

2. HTTP-Based C2

Most modern botnets employ HTTP or HTTPS protocols for C2, blending in as typical web traffic to evade discovery. Bots regularly "check in" with a web server for commands, updates, or payloads.

Pros:

- Blends with ordinary web traffic, evading firewalls and intrusion detection systems.
- Can be encrypted using HTTPS to hide content.

Cons:

- Remains dependent on a central server, which can be deny-listed or taken down offline through law enforcement and judicial channels.

3. Peer-to-Peer (P2P) C2

To enhance resilience, some botnets employ P2P networks where one bot communicates with a limited set of peers. Commands pass through this peer network, avoiding dependence on a single server.

Pros:

- No single point of failure.
- No solitary target to eliminate.
- Harder to dismantle and trace.

Cons:

- More difficult to construct and operate.

- Slower communication throughout the network.

4. Other well-known Protocols (TCP/UDP)

Other types of common application-layer protocols, such as SQL, NTP, etc. are commonly used across standard TCP or UDP ports to masquerade as legitimate applications. To evade deep-packet inspection, these communication channels are often compressed, encrypted, or padded with obfuscatory data to conceal their content and patterns from security analysis.

Pros:

- Masquerading malicious traffic over usual ports and novel packet formats that avoid detection by signature-based intrusion detection systems.

Cons:

- Reverse-engineering the network packets itself can provide defenders with useful information, and anomaly-detection systems may notice anomalies or odd packet sizes.

Motivations and Botnet Actors

Every botnet has a purpose, and it's critical to understand who builds them and why they are built to anticipate and prevent their use. In general, there are three main types of actors who drive botnet activity: financially motivated criminals, hacktivists, and state-sponsored actors.

1. Financial Gain

Most botnets are made for profit, first and foremost. Botnets are monetized in a number of different ways:

- DDoS-for-hire (booter/stresser) services, which allow users to pay for launching an attack against competitors.
- Spam distribution, such as phishing campaigns or ad fraud.
- Credential theft for identity theft or account hijack.

These profit-driven actors pose as businesses that develop sophisticated malware, offer customer support, and even advertise botnet access on darknet websites.

2. Hacktivism

Hacktivists are people driven by ideology who employ botnets to further ideological or social agendas. They typically target governments, businesses, or other entities that they perceive to be oppressive or unjust.

For instance, the infamous collective Anonymous used DDoS powered by botnets to protest fraud and censorship. Such activity, while illegal, is frequently repositioned by offenders as digital civil disobedience.

3. State-Sponsored Activities

Nation-state actors employ botnets for cyber spying, infrastructure interruption, and psychological warfare. These types of activities usually involve the use of highly advanced botnets that are used for a longer term and are difficult to detect.

These actors can employ botnets for:

- Disrupting competitor economies.
- Collecting intelligence.
- Launch simultaneous attacks during periods of geopolitical unrest.

Examples are the use of botnets in the Russia-Ukraine conflict and the alleged involvement of Chinese botnets in intellectual property theft targeting Western businesses.

In every instance, the anonymity and the scale available with botnets make them appealing weapons for a diverse cast of malicious actors, each pursuing different objectives yet capable of inflicting equally severe harm

Conventional Tools: Antivirus and Patch Management – Their Limitations and Evolution

For decades, antivirus software and patch management solutions have been the primary defenses against malware infections and botnet proliferation. While still important for cybersecurity, these tools are increasingly proving inadequate against today's sophisticated attacks.

Antivirus Software

Classic antivirus software is mostly dependent on signature-based detection, identifying known malware by comparing it to a database of virus definitions. Though good at protecting against previously known malware, this approach has difficulties with:

- Zero-day exploits, attacks that are based on vulnerabilities that the software builder and developers are unaware of.
- Polymorphic malware, which changes its code in order to avoid detection.
- Fileless malware, which resides in memory and does not leave any footprint on disk.

Furthermore, most antivirus tools require regular updates and regular system scans, which can consume significant resources and often experience delays, allowing fast-spreading threats like botnet malware to bypass detection.

Patch Management

Patch management involves keeping software and firmware up-to-date to address known vulnerabilities. Although it is critical, patch management faces various challenges:

- Delays in deploying patches due to operational risks, compatibility issues, or a lack of automation.
- Decentralized environments, especially with IoT devices, where updates are either unavailable or difficult to deploy.

- User resistance or negligence, particularly in consumer devices, where security is often an afterthought.

As threats have progressed, so have these tools. Modern solutions today include behavioral analysis, heuristics, machine learning, and vulnerability scanning that is automated. Despite their advances, traditional tools are only one layer of a broader, multi-tier defense and are no longer sufficient on their own to counter today's botnet-driven DDoS attacks.

Emerging Frontier: Smart Devices Duality as Assets and Liabilities

The proliferation of smart devices, from industrial sensors and autonomous automobiles to virtual assistants and smart televisions, signifies a radical shift in the way we interact with technology. Smart gadgets are a valuable asset for homes, businesses, and infrastructure systems because they provide effectiveness, automated processes, and data-enabled cognition.

But their hasty proliferation has opened a parallel frontier of cybersecurity threats. Much of these smart devices are constructed with little regard for security, frequently with default credentials, unsecured protocols, and minimal update regimes. Once installed, they may be hard or impossible to upgrade, particularly in broad-scale or distant deployments.

From the botnet viewpoint, smart devices are perfect targets:

- They are constantly connected, offering steady availability for malicious exploitation.

- They're usually low-profile; victims might not even know they've been hacked.
- Their processing power, as small as it is per device, aggregates into something powerful.

Take the Mirai botnet, a classic case, it harnessed a thousand-strong army of insecurely configured IoT devices to commit one of the largest DDoS attacks ever. It highlighted the two-sided nature of intelligent devices: as instruments of innovation and as doorways to cyber abuse.

As we look towards a more interconnected future, it is essential to treat smart devices as assets and liabilities. Security needs to be built in, not an afterthought, to protect their vast potential.

Automating Vulnerability Management in Distributed Device Environments

Today, organizations often operate across decentralized networks of endpoints, including cloud servers, mobile devices, and IoT systems. This challenge has made automation a cornerstone of modern vulnerability management.

Automated vulnerability management systems perform a continuous set of tasks for:

- Asset discovery – detecting all connected devices and systems.

- Vulnerability scanning – detection of known weaknesses based on CVEs and misconfiguration.
- Risk prioritization – ordering issues by severity, exploitability, and asset value.
- Remediation or mitigation – initiating automated patch deployment or configuration modifications.

Traditional software tools from Qualys, Rapid7, Tenable, and from open-source implementations such as OpenVAS have matured to provide real-time scanning, integration into patch management systems, and reporting dashboards.

Automation in distributed settings ensures that:

- Security policies are uniformly enforced geographically and by device.
- High-priority vulnerabilities are resolved quickly, minimizing windows of exposure.
- Human mistakes are kept to a minimum, and the utilization of resources is optimized.

Streamlining vulnerability management is not only economical, but also essential to provide active, strong cyber defence as threat actors keep targeting dispersed systems.

Chapter 3: ISP-Level View of DDoS

Effect on ISP Infrastructure

Internet Service Providers (ISPs) function on a vast scale, serving as the infrastructure of international connectivity. Each second, they handle billions of packets of data through a convoluted network of switches, routers, and transit locations to provide smooth communication for millions of clients. At this scale, they are not only essential infrastructure but also very lucrative targets for Distributed Denial of Service (DDoS) attacks.

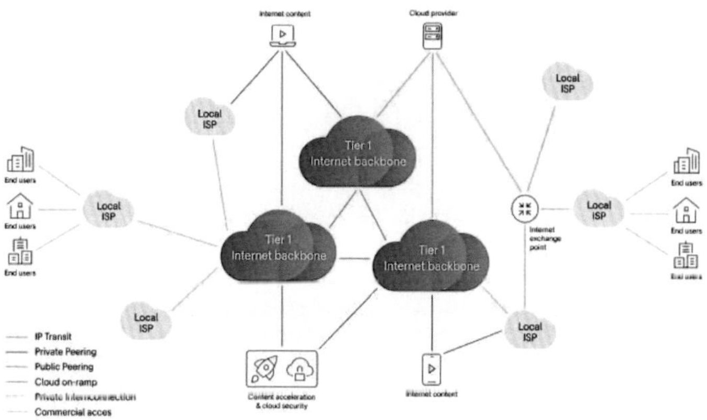

Ref: Arelion.com

Image: When a user browses to an internet site, this network traffic may transit through multiple ISP hops before reaching its target.

DDoS attacks are meant to drain system resources, and against ISPs, they hit the most basic layer of internet connectivity, bandwidth, and routing infrastructure. Attackers swamp the ISP's network with an incredible amount of malicious traffic, usually stemming from enormous botnets made up of hacked devices located worldwide. The volume of the attack is so massive that it can fill up available bandwidth, starving legitimate traffic from passing through.

One of the earliest signs of a successful DDoS attack against an ISP is bandwidth saturation. Similar to traffic congestion on a freeway, when data packets come pouring in all at once, the network clogs up. The throughput available is used up quickly, slowing down or completely shutting off service for everyone relying on that portion of the network. Even a modest volume of well-targeted traffic can have disproportionate effects owing to the interconnectivity of the routing paths.

After congestion, router overload becomes a serious problem. ISPs use high-capacity routers to facilitate packet flow and route information through several nodes at optimal rates. However, these routers have limited processing capacity and memory. When subjected to the pressure of receiving millions of packets per second, several of which are malformed or spoofed, the routers can crash or get into fail-safe modes, further degrading the quality of service.

This domino effect not only hits the targeted ISP but also hits downstream clients and even other ISPs that are connected through peering arrangements. Businesses that depend on uninterrupted bandwidth suffer outages, VoIP users suffer dropped calls, stock trading is interrupted in financial platforms, and cloud services experience performance degradation.

ISPs' extensive reach is a double-edged sword. While their geographically diverse routes, terabits of backbone capacity, and on-net scrubbing centres provide a built-in buffer against volumetric floods, their size additionally demonstrates numerous routers, peering links, and customer edges that an intruder could exploit. The asymmetric economics of contemporary DDoS, where attackers can affordably unlock traffic bursts which outweigh any single link, necessitate that providers continuously improve identification, screening, and fail-over strategies to maintain the resilience of the internet's backbone, despite the fact that these networks are designed for high availability.

Challenges in Detection and Mitigation

Detection and prevention of DDoS attacks at the ISP level is perhaps one of the most technically daunting challenges in network security. The very nature of DDoS attacks, distributed, burdensome, and frequently masquerading as regular traffic, predisposes them to be hidden until extensive harm has been done. ISPs are required to walk a fine line: blocking malicious data without stifling legitimate traffic.

Central to the issue is the difficulty of separating malicious traffic from legitimate traffic. Attackers generally make use of methods imitating actual user activity, including Slowloris or HTTP floods that look like normal browsing sessions. For ISPs, this complicates the reliance on conventional pattern-matching or rule-based mechanisms. Additionally, most attacks now come from compromised machines that often do not follow obvious suspicious patterns of behavior. Rather, they become camouflaged in the network "noise," their detection being dependent on slight behavioral anomalies and traffic baselines that are different per customer and times of day.

Real-time filtering is another challenge. ISPs typically process terabits per second of traffic, and it's not feasible to examine every packet in detail. Inline filtering products, like firewalls or scrubbing devices, tend to add latency and may themselves become a bottleneck. Additionally, most internet traffic nowadays is encrypted with sophisticated cryptographic protocols making it almost impossible to conduct a complete traffic inspection. In high-speed networks, use of cloud-based solutions for mitigation lead to a higher degree of latency which negatively affects user experience. Any kind of network-level filtering needs to strike a balance between speed and accuracy, particularly during volumetric attacks.

This leads us to the question of sensitivity vs. false positives. If an ISP sets its detection systems for high sensitivity, it may detect and block genuine surges in traffic, such as flash sales, live sports, or viral content, as possible attacks. If detection thresholds are too loose, genuine DDoS attacks pass undetected. This is not a one-time calibration; it requires continuous tuning, adaptive thresholds, and regular feedback from network analysts.

One problem that is especially frustrating is that of stealth attacks and adaptive evasion. Botnets no longer are the loud, hammer-away machines of yesteryear. They are sophisticated, able to change attack vectors mid-course, spread load across thousands of IP addresses, and make use of encrypted streams to cover their payloads. Some botnets employ "low and slow" strategies, causing minimal traffic from each bot but collectively battering a target over time. It's challenging to differentiate these attacks from standard user behavior, especially when dispersed across shared ports or cloud providers.

Advanced evasion techniques also encompass IP spoofing, rapid-flux DNS to regularly change attack sources, and packet fragmentation to bypass signature-based detection. In most scenarios, ISPs are forced to leverage heuristics, anomaly scoring, and traffic modeling to detect threats in real-time. These solutions are highly resource-intensive and also remain susceptible to evasion.

In short, the ISP challenge is not just technical, it's also strategic. ISPs have to counter an enemy that's in constant flux, frequently indistinguishable from expected legit network traffic, and scaled in size to match the ISP's own infrastructure. Detection and mitigation are therefore not one-off solutions but ongoing processes requiring smart automation, expert human management, and inter-industry cooperation.

Legal and Ethical Responsibilities

Internet Service Providers occupy a privileged position in the online universe: they are both facilitators of connectivity and protectors of internet traffic. Therefore, they have important legal and ethical obligations in determining, precluding, and reacting to DDoS attacks. These obligations, though, differ widely among jurisdictions and tend to lie in legal borderlands, especially when they need to balance security against user privacy.

In most regions of the world, ISPs are legally required to use reasonable steps to secure their facilities and prevent customer disruption of service. In the European Union, for instance, the NIS2 Directive obligates "essential" providers of a service such as ISPs to put in place technical and organizational measures to ensure that cybersecurity risks are effectively managed. Likewise, the FCC in the US requires ISPs to keep networks up and running reliably and can hold them liable if negligence causes mass outages.

These laws often stop short of prescribing how ISPs must detect or mitigate DDoS threats. There is considerable ambiguity regarding surveillance rights, data retention, and the use of deep packet inspection. This generates a legal grey area: ISPs need to snoop on traffic to detect malicious activity, but they do not want to infringe on data protection regulations like the General Data Protection Regulation (GDPR) in Europe or state-level privacy laws in the US.

On an international level, the strategies for ISP accountability are diverse. In countries such as China and Russia, ISPs are under tight state control and are regularly obliged to report and block suspicious traffic right away. However, liberal democracies have a focus on privacy for users and impose higher levels of transparency and accountability on surveillance habits. This difference poses difficulties for multi-national ISPs that have to contend with inconsistent legal requisites across borders.

Ethically, ISPs are caught between customer privacy and proactive defense. In order to spot stealthy DDoS patterns or botnet activity, ISPs can potentially have to inspect behavioral trends, log connection metadata, or mark certain IP addresses, all of which can open the door to surveillance and abuse concerns. It's even more sensitive when governments ask ISPs to disclose this information for law enforcement or intelligence purposes.

Ultimately, ISPs have to tread a thin tightrope: they should be defending their networks and customers from harm, but also protect privacy rights, remain neutral, and not overreach. To navigate this balance, major ISPs are implementing transparency reports, ethics review boards, and privacy-by-design principles, showing that effective cybersecurity can and ought to coexist with respect for civil liberties.

Limitations of Traditional ISP Infrastructure

Even though they form the linchpin of global connectivity, most Internet Service Providers still run on infrastructure that was never created to manage the size or dynamic nature of advanced cyber threats such as DDoS attacks.

One major constraint is the old hardware still entrenched in most ISP networks. Routers and switches installed several years back might not have the processing power or the memory size to support terabit-scale traffic when doing deep packet analysis or behavioral inspection. Such legacy devices were designed for throughput and reliability rather than security-focused operations like anomaly detection or rate limiting at wire speed. Consequently, they are bottlenecks in case of volumetric DDoS attacks or just don't possess the capabilities necessary to contribute to a contemporary defense strategy.

Aside from hardware limitations, most ISPs continue to employ strict routing practices and static traffic engineering concepts. BGP (Border Gateway Protocol), the network protocol used by all service providers to share routing information, is not designed for dynamic threat containment. Route reconfiguration to counter an active DDoS attack is not only time-consuming but can result in cascading and unforeseen ripple effects throughout the network, impacting legitimate traffic patterns and peering relationships.

Scalability is also a fundamental issue. Legacy infrastructure does not have the elasticity to respond to traffic spikes, whether due to genuine spikes or attacks. Without automated scaling or cloud-based augmentation, ISPs might be unable to provide a good quality of service during even relatively small DDoS incidents.

Adding to these technical constraints are operational issues. Most ISPs continue to use traditional monitoring tools and rule-driven alert systems that create huge volumes of alerts with little context. This creates alert fatigue, where network operations centers (NOCs) that are already stretched become deluged by noise, unable to focus on true threats. In the absence of intelligent correlation or triage systems, groups find themselves being reactive, not proactive.

In addition, the absence of automation is time-constraining. In most instances, network administrators are required to reroute traffic manually, block IPs offending the network, or spin up scrubbing centers manually. Manual processes are prone to error and too slow to counteract rapidly moving DDoS campaigns effectively.

Finally, there is a skills gap. Preventing modern cyber-attacks necessitates expert-level knowledge in areas such as threat intelligence, DDoS detection, and automated mitigation. Numerous ISP teams, particularly within mid-market or regional providers, might be inadequately trained or under-staffed, thereby facing difficulties in incorporating bleeding-edge defenses.

All these constraints underpin the reason why upgrading ISP infrastructure is not merely about hardware upgrades, it's about changing organizational processes, developing in-house talent and hiring quality staff, and adopting automation in order to stay robust in a hostile digital landscape.

Traffic Scrubbing at ISP Level

Traffic scrubbing is an imperative security measure employed by ISPs to counter huge-scale DDoS attacks. Traffic scrubbing redirects network traffic to special infrastructure, typically consisting of scrubbing centers, where malicious data packets are detected and eliminated before redirecting the clean traffic to its destination. This process is unavoidable since standard network devices such as routers and switches cannot analyze and filter huge amounts of potentially harmful traffic in real time.

Scrubbing is required whenever an ISP is hit by volumetric attacks that outgrow the bandwidth or processing power of its routing equipment. Instead of sending this traffic directly to the customer or to the core network, it is routed to a scrubbing center where sophisticated filtering methodologies are practiced. These consist of packet examination, rate limiting, protocol checking, and anomaly detection. The aim is to separate legitimate traffic from attack traffic without incurring too much disturbance on regular services.

Major ISPs and CDN (Content Delivery Network) operators usually have a worldwide network of scrubbing centers positioned to maximize low latency and high availability. These scrubbing centers are provisioned with high-end hardware and have integrated real-time threat feeds. Traffic is diverted, whether manually or automatically, to the local scrubbing center when a DDoS attack is identified using techniques such as traffic monitoring, threat feeds, and signature-based detections.

Scrubbing may be used in two primary modes: inline filtering and out-of-path filtering. Under inline filtering, traffic is routed through the scrubbing by default, permitting constant monitoring but subjecting it to extra latency. Under out-of-path filtering, traffic is made to pass through the scrubbing center only upon the detection of an attack. This method reduces latency during normal circumstances but requires real-time detection and rerouting abilities in the event of an attack.

Although very effective, traffic scrubbing has its operational and cost trade-offs. Since it requires specialised gear, bandwidth, and human resources, its maintenance is expensive. Specifically for real-time applications like VoIP and internet gaming where milliseconds matter, the delay may negatively impact an application's performance, and also leads to degraded user experience.

In spite of all these challenges, traffic scrubbing continues to be the foundation of ISP-grade DDoS protection. As volumetric and sophisticated attacks increase, scrubbing centers are being innovated with automation and real time traffic inspection, allowing for faster, better mitigation with less human involvement. For ISPs, it is no longer a choice, but a necessity to invest in solid scrubbing capabilities to maintain uptime, customer faith, and network integrity.

Information Sharing Among ISPs

As DDoS attacks are global in scope, so should the defences against them. Mitigation of these attacks is enhanced through collaboration and information sharing across ISPs because DDoS traffic often comes from thousands of different locations across many networks.

Another prominent effort is the establishment of Information Sharing and Analysis Centers (ISACs). These industry-specific organizations, like the Communications ISAC or Financial Services ISAC (FS-ISAC), enable the efficient sharing of threat intelligence, attack signatures, and live indicators of compromise (IOCs). If an ISP identifies a new DDoS pattern type or command-and-control signature, it can immediately notify others, reducing the spread and impact of the attack.

Numerous instances of cooperative takedown and mitigation efforts have been documented. ISPs, cloud providers, and security researchers collaborated to sinkhole malicious domains and block access to compromised devices during the 2016 coordinated disassembly of the Mirai botnet infrastructure.

ISPs also participate in peering arrangements, permitting efficient traffic exchange between networks. ISPs can distribute IP addresses or prefixes associated with identified botnets sources among several networks by using these agreements to exchange deny-lists. Collective defence is further enhanced by new signalling protocols, such as DDoS Open Threat Signalling, which allow systems to share DDoS mitigation requests automatically and in real time.

In effect, cooperation multiplies defense. By coordinating on standards, sharing intelligence, and coordinating response actions, ISPs can take what would otherwise be disjointed vulnerabilities and create a robust, distributed shield against one of the most enduring threats on the internet.

Chapter 4: Application-Level View of DDoS

Introduction to Application-Layer DDoS Attacks

Volumetric and protocol-based DDoS attacks endeavor to saturate and congest network infrastructure, whereas application-layer DDoS attacks aim to assault a web application server. Application-layer DDoS attacks function at Layer 7 of the OSI model, targeting the way applications handle requests as opposed to network processing of the internet traffic.

Application-layer attacks spoof and mimic the behavior of legitimate users, making them more difficult to identify using traditional network defense tools. A good example is the Slowloris attack, where an attacker sends incomplete HTTP requests at very slow rates, opening up connections and consuming server resources without ever finishing them. This gradually drains the server of the ability to process new connections. Another widely used vector is the HTTP flood, where attackers send large amounts of seemingly legitimate HTTP GET or POST requests to the application. These can lead to database straining, CPU overloading, and timeouts for legitimate users. SQL injection, a well known yet commonly found exploitation vector, can also be used to DDoS a website by creating resource-intensive queries that consume a lot of backend resources, effectively shutting down the application.

What sets these attacks apart from network-layer DDoS is not traffic volume but their intent and effect. While a network DDoS might swamp a firewall or internet pipe with a high volume of traffic, an application-layer attack can overwhelm a weak endpoint even with a few requests per second. They are thus a weapon of choice for attackers who want to circumvent traditional DDoS protection methods.

Learning about application-layer DDoS attacks is key to cybersecurity planning. They can be a low-bandwidth, high-impact danger, taking advantage of defects and software bugs within the logic, configuration, or architecture of an application. Their capacity for maximum damage with minimal bandwidth makes them both threatening and hard to detect.

Impact on Availability and Business Continuity

The impact of an application-layer DDoS attack extends far beyond mere technical disruption; it can attack a business's very operations, reputation, and trust. While wider network-level floods may target multiple systems indiscriminately, application-layer attacks can be precisely aimed, toppling mission-critical services with pinpoint accuracy.

User experience is usually the initial and most obvious victim. Applications can degrade to unusable speeds, timeout on simple operations, or be completely unavailable. For e-commerce websites, this results in lost sales during critical times. For SaaS vendors, it results in angry customers, higher churn, and support congestion. Even measured in minutes, downtime can create major ripple effects.

Aside from technical hassle, there is also a financial impact. Protracted outages can lead to direct revenue loss, higher operational expenses incurred from response to the incidents, and regulatory penalties if SLAs are violated. Secondary loss factors are losses in customer confidence, damage to brand reputation, and negative publicity, particularly if the company is viewed as unprepared or careless.

For very visible businesses, particularly those in finance, healthcare, or government, reputational harm can linger. Trust once lost is difficult to recover when users doubt the stability or safety of an application. Such times can provide opportunities for competitors to poach customers based on perceived vulnerabilities.

In addition, application-layer attacks are frequently used as smokescreens for more substantial intrusions. While the IT and security staff is occupied to restore services, attackers may be testing other vulnerabilities or installing malware. This double-threat character adds to the need for thorough defense and business continuity planning.

In a world where digital presence is equated with business viability, defending against application-layer DDoS is not an IT issue; it's a business imperative.

Typical application design flaws

Most applications unwittingly expose themselves to DDoS risks through poor design decisions. In contrast to infrastructure defences, application-level robustness has to be incorporated into the architecture at the beginning. Too often, this does not happen as security is an after-thought at most organizations.

One major weakness is the absence of input validation. User inputs that are not sanitised or bounded can be used by attackers to create requests which use up the excessive resources of the server. For instance, submitting malformed or highly nested JSON payloads can slowly ramp up the processing time, wasting CPU cycles and inducing latency throughout the system.

Inadequate session management is also an underappreciated problem. Programs that don't establish good session timeouts or permit unlimited login attempts can leave server resources reserved much longer than needed. The attackers take advantage by creating many sessions which remain in memory, filling up server-side session storage and affecting all users.

And then there are bandwidth-intensive endpoints, APIs or URLs that execute costly operations such as deep database queries, huge file downloads, or real-time analytics. Unless these endpoints are rate-limited or cached, they are sitting ducks. Attackers simply automate requests to these costly paths, rapidly exhausting server bandwidth, memory, or storage I/O.

All together, these vulnerabilities create a rich attack surface for application-layer DDoS. Much of the time, the issue isn't an attacker's power; it's the weakness of the application. Protection at this level demands that software development teams communicate extensively with security engineers, so each feature is developed with resource frugality, security and resilience in its focus.

OWASP Top Ten risk is the most serious security threat for web applications, such as -

- Broken Access Control – Users are able to access data or functions they are not supposed to.
- Cryptographic Failures – Important data is not securely protected due to poor encryption.
- Injection – Tricky input is executed as code, causing attacks such as SQL injection.
- Insecure Design – Flawed security design decisions result in exploitable vulnerabilities.
- Security Misconfiguration – Inadvertent settings leave systems vulnerable.
- Vulnerable and Outdated Components – Implementing outdated libraries or software presents known threats.
- Identification and Authentication Failures – Poor login systems enable unauthorized access.
- Software and Data Integrity Failures – Code or data can be manipulated because integrity checks are missing.
- Security Logging and Monitoring Failures – No logging and alerting causes delays in detecting breaches.

Server-Side Request Forgery (SSRF) – Attackers cause servers to issue unauthorized requests to internal systems.

Challenges in Mitigating Application-Layer DDoS

Mitigating against application-layer DDoS attacks is fundamentally more challenging than blocking brute-force network floods. The attacks are covert, targeted, and obfuscated, making mitigation both technically challenging and operationally sensitive.

A fundamental problem is coping with newer data request patterns. Attackers tend to emulate normal user behaviour: reading pages, filling out forms, querying databases. There's no glaring traffic volume spike, no invalid packets, just an astronomical volume of "legitimate" requests. Even conventional DDoS protection, such as rate-based limits or IP blocking, tends to be ineffective here since it is not able to distinguish at this level between abusive and normal behavior.

This brings us directly into the second issue of importance: difficulty in identifying legitimate users. Most application-layer attacks come from distributed botnets with residential proxies or hijacked machines, masquerading as real users with real IPs. Some even mimic human-like behavior, page-flipping, waiting for random intervals, or execute JavaScript to better circumvent bot detection controls.

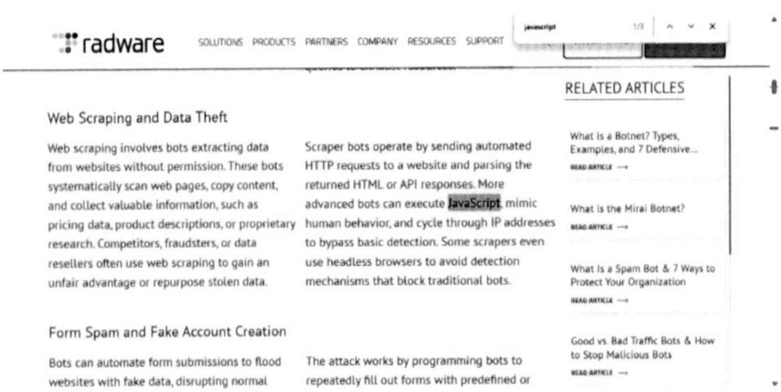

Compounding the challenge is the requirement for real-time response. After an attack begins to manifest as a degradation in user experience, seconds matter. But response items such as manual firewall blocks or access revocations tend to trail behind, while proactive defenses have to find a delicate balance not to block valid users. Overly aggressive mitigation can be as detrimental to business as the attack itself.

Then there's the operational overhead. Application-layer defenses require looking into observability logs, metrics, traces and connecting to wider security platforms. Not all organisations have the infrastructure or capabilities to stand up such a multi-layered defense.

Ultimately, preventing these attacks involves intelligent detection, flexible defenses, and close collaboration among development, DevOps, and security groups. It's not just about scaling the infrastructure; it's about knowing when something is "off" even when it appears entirely normal.

Secure Coding and Vulnerability Management

Preventing application-layer DDoS starts not with firewalls or rate limiters, but with secure code. Most DDoS vulnerabilities are rooted in logic errors, poor processing, or unbounded input processing, all of which can and must be dealt with carefully during the software development process. This is where the concept of "shift-left security" applies.

Shift-left security involves embedding security practices early in the software development life cycle (SDLC) as opposed to bolt-on approaches later. By including threat modelling, secure design reviews, static code analysis and other application security practices up front, teams will be able to identify DDoS-relevant vulnerabilities before they get deployed to production. This forward-looking strategy lessens both the cost and risk of future occurrences.

One of the pillars of this approach is Secure DevOps (DevSecOps), integrating security controls into the CI/CD pipeline. Methods such as dynamic application security testing (DAST), software composition analysis (SCA), fuzzing, and test coverage for high-resource endpoints ensure each release is examined for possible abuse vectors. Configuration management tools can also enforce best practices for resource assignment, timeout limits, and error handling.

Routine vulnerability management augments secure coding. This encompasses scanning software libraries for identified CVEs, patching old components, and monitoring third-party APIs or integrations that can act as indirect DDoS gateways.

In the end, preventing application-layer DDoS is not about writing secure code; it's about building a secure development culture where developers, testers, and security teams collaborate to develop strong systems from the start.

Real-World Case Studies

The potential threat of application-layer DDoS attacks becomes more real when we look at actual events. A number of high-profile attacks demonstrate how much damage these attacks can cause and how various organizations reacted.

Case 1: Financial Services Firm – API Flood Attack

In June 2021, a financial services provider was targeted with a massive multi-vector DDoS attack that reached a peak volume of 840 Gbps, according to a case study published by F5 Labs. The attack included SYN floods, RST floods, UDP reflection, and ICMP floods, and originated from clients across 42 countries. Remarkably, legitimate traffic (approximately 25 Mbps) was largely unaffected, but the sheer amplification, up to 33,600X normal traffic, suggests substantial strain on backend systems even with high bandwidth and generic DDoS protections in place.

Case 2: E-Commerce Platforms – Black Friday Preparedness

During peak shopping events like Black Friday and Cyber Monday, e-commerce platforms face dramatic traffic surges. For example, Platform.sh reported a 65% increase in traffic on Black Friday 2024 compared to other Fridays that year, and a 14% increase over Black Friday 2023. That same year, Adobe estimated $10.8 billion in online sales occurred on Black Friday in the U.S., up from $9.8 billion in 2023.

To manage these surges, many retailers deploy auto-scaling infrastructures and prioritize performance testing. SCAYLE noted that it processed 128% more growth during Black Friday 2024 compared to the prior year, achieved by running early load tests, freezing code before the event, reserving extra compute capacity (e.g., via AWS), and monitoring critical systems in real time.

Furthermore, bot attacks pose a significant threat during these periods. Radware reported that in the weeks leading up to Black Friday 2024, a major e-commerce client faced over 1 billion price-scraping bot attempts over a 30-day stretch, averaging 45 million attempts daily. Consequently, e-commerce operations frequently employ rate limiting, CAPTCHA or bot-detection systems, centralized observability, and real-time traffic profiling to mitigate both adversarial bot threats and infrastructure strain.

Both of these stories teach a valuable lesson: Application-layer DDoS resilience is primarily an architectural and operational property, not something you can bolt on with a single tool or setting.

What breaks is usually brittle back-end logic and poor monitoring. What succeeds is layered defense, forward-thinking engineering, and adherence to secure design principles.

Rate Limiting, CAPTCHAs, Challenge-Response

One of the easiest measures against application-layer DDoS is rate limiting, limiting the requests a user or an IP can initiate within a specified time interval. It counters volumetric floods aimed at individual endpoints, particularly those involving high backend processing. Well-tuned rate limits can be user role-based, IP geolocation-based, or behavior pattern–based, while remaining flexible without inconveniencing legitimate users.

To block spurious traffic, CAPTCHAs act as a challenge-response system, expecting users to complete puzzles that are typically challenging for traditional bots to deal with. They are not perfect, but they increase the attack cost and discourage less advanced bots.

JavaScript challenges and progressive delays are additional effective techniques. This entail checking the client's script-processing capability or slowing down responses intentionally following repeated requests, both of which reveal bots attempting to act at scale. When executed properly, these multiple strategies present a solid buffer against low-and-slow and high-frequency attacks.

Web Application Firewalls (WAFs)

WAFs, which sit between the user and the server, apply configurable sets of rules to block identified risks in real-time, and monitor inbound HTTP/HTTPS traffic for malicious activity.

New-generation WAFs also offer signature-based detection, which recognises known attack payloads (such as SQL injection patterns), and behavioral analysis, which detects anomalies in request frequency, header format, or access patterns. This dual feature is essential in detecting both brute-force and stealth DDoS attempts.

Most cloud-based WAFs include auto-updating rule sets calibrated through global threat feeds. This keeps the system up to date to respond to emerging threats. Integration with application logic enables WAFs to be aware of context, allowing or denying access based on user activity, session integrity, or geo-IP location.

Utilized properly, a WAF not only prevents attacks but also eliminates alert fatigue by blocking background noise and delivering only actionable threats to incident response teams.

Auto-Scaling and Cloud Resilience

One of the major benefits of cloud infrastructure is the ability to auto-scale, adjusting computing resources dynamically in response to real-time demand. During DDoS attacks, auto-scaling enables applications to handle surges in traffic without degrading performance, at least on a temporary basis.

When experiencing a spike, load balancers send incoming requests to newly created instances, avoiding bottlenecks. Stateless microservices are particularly suitable for this pattern as they can be scaled horizontally with little configuration overhead.

Nevertheless, auto-scaling is not a panacea. It is most effective when accompanied by rate limiting and attack detection to prevent resource exhaustion attacks, where the attacker attempts to cause cost overruns or exhaust service limits. Scaling thresholds must be set cautiously by defenders, and monitoring must be performed for indications of artificial demand.

Auto-scaling, properly configured, changes the infrastructure from a static target to an elastic buffer zone, allowing organizations additional time to observe, analyze, and react to application-layer DDoS attempts.

CDN Protection (e.g., Cloudflare, Fastly, Akamai)

Content Delivery Networks (CDNs) such as Cloudflare and Akamai are crucial for application-layer DDoS protection as they act as a distributed layer between users and the origin server, absorbing, filtering, and distributing malicious traffic before it ever reaches the application itself. CDNs cache static content near users and scan incoming requests for malicious patterns.

Their globally-available infrastructure has inherent redundancy and scale, making it hard for attackers to overload any one node. CDNs also provide integrated WAFs, bot protection, and real-time analytics. CDNs filter, absorb, and geo-disperse attack traffic and work as both a shield and an early warning system for application-layer DDoS attacks.

Monitoring and Logging (ELK, Prometheus, Grafana)

No defense plan is finished without thorough observability. Strong log collecting and analysis is provided by solutions like ELK Stack (Elasticsearch, Logstash, Kibana), which enables teams to find irregularities in user behaviour, request patterns, or error rates.

Grafana, after gathering Prometheus metrics, enables real-time visual monitoring of application performance metrics and indicators, such as CPU utilisation, request count, HTTP error rates, and request latency. These make it possible to quickly identify, escalate, and stop application-layer DDoS attacks actively. Alerts can be set up on these metrics through Grafana, and connectors can be used to send notifications when an SLA is breached for quick actions.

Chapter 5: DDoS Detection Techniques for ISPs

Introduction to ISP-Level Detection

Internet Service Providers (ISPs) have a unique and powerful role in the cybersecurity landscape. Serving as the backbone of internet connectivity, they not only forward traffic across the global network but also serve as the first line of defense against mass-scale Distributed Denial of Service (DDoS) attacks. Their strategic location not only gives them unparalleled visibility into vast quantities of traffic, but also puts them squarely in charge of being able to see and react to attacks before they spread into downstream outages.

Compared to enterprise or application-level defense, detection at the ISP level is infinitely more difficult. The sheer volume of traffic, combined with the diversity of protocols and the dynamic nature of traffic flows, makes deep inspection both technically challenging and expensive in terms of both cost and performance. This complexity is further compounded by the rise of encrypted traffic, IP spoofing, and botnet obfuscation techniques, which significantly reduce the effectiveness of traditional detection methods.

At times, the detection process can be more difficult than the mitigation process. While both mitigation and detection must be timely, accurate, and scalable, effective mitigation is only possible when backed by high-quality detection. Techniques like traffic scrubbing or null routing are powerful mitigation tools, but their success hinges on how accurately and quickly threats are identified. As a result, ISPs must invest heavily in developing robust, intelligent detection workflows that can feed actionable insights into mitigation systems. ISPs must monitor traffic in near-real time, tens or hundreds of terabits per second, so full-packet inspection is not possible. They thus use flow-based analysis and statistical models. These methods can provide early warning indicators but come with their own limitations and trade-offs.

Traffic Monitoring Protocols: NetFlow and IPFIX

Effective detection of DDoS on the ISP level hinges on understanding traffic patterns, what is normal, what is abnormal, and what indicates an active attack. ISPs accomplish this using flow monitoring protocols like NetFlow, sFlow, and IPFIX. They don't inspect all packets but only certain samples to collect information about network flows, IP address conversations over time, to build a profile of the behavior of the network.

Cisco created NetFlow, a program that records flow data across switches and routers. Important metadata like source and destination IP addresses, ports, protocol category, packet and byte counts, and timestamps are all contained in the record. Security experts may monitor usage trends, spot volumetric irregularities, and spot any command-and-control channels or scans thanks to the gathered information.

IPFIX (IP Flow Information Export) is an IETF-standardized extension of NetFlow. It extends NetFlow's functionality with support for customizable fields and vendor-independent implementation, thus making it a fit for many different network environments aside from Cisco infrastructure.

Gathering the sampled flow data comes with its own set of challenges. Instead of generating a NetFlow record for every single packet, sampling involves collecting data for only a subset of packets. This is typically expressed as a ratio, e.g., 1:100 means that 1 out of every 100 packets is sampled and contributes to NetFlow records. A high sampling rate consumes less resources, but comes at the cost of less granularity about the network flows. Higher the sampling rate, the greater the risk of overlooking quiet, low-rate DDoS attacks. Conversely, capturing high-resolution data offers superior detection capabilities but at the cost of increased demands on storage, processing, and network resources.

Hybrid approaches are most commonly used in production ISP environments. sFlow, a packet sampling protocol that captures both packet headers and interface counters, is typically used to monitor access or edge points due to its lightweight design and real-time capabilities. In contrast, NetFlow/IPFIX focus on flow records and provide more detailed flow-level metadata, making them better suited for backbone routers where flow context is essential. Used together, these protocols constitute the eyes of a network, supplying the raw data needed to drive detection algorithms and feed analysis platforms.

Though they have their shortcomings, flow protocols remain the backbone of ISP-level detection. To function, they depend on thoughtful placement, smart configuration, and seamless integration with detection infrastructure capable of interpreting raw flows into useful notifications.

Signature-Based Detection vs. Behavioral Analysis

Signature-based detection relies on recognized patterns or "signatures" of attack traffic. Such signatures may be recognized IP addresses, payload structures, port number sequences, or abuses of known protocols. Like antivirus software, once an attack vector is characterized, it can be precisely detected by comparing any incoming traffic against this database. This method excels at the rapid detection of known threats with high accuracy and minimal false positives.

But signature-based systems are inherently reactive; they only know to search for what they've seen before. In the era of polymorphic attacks and zero-day DDoS vectors, attackers can bypass these systems with careful modifications in their approach.

Unlike traditional methods that rely on known attack signatures, behavioral analysis builds a baseline of typical network behavior. This includes learning normal traffic volumes, how protocols are used, timing patterns, and flow characteristics. When network activity deviates from this established "normal," it triggers an alert. It uses heuristics like unusual spikes in volume, changes in data randomness (entropy), or abnormal access patterns to spot suspicious activities, including zero-day and adaptive attacks.

While behavioral systems are more agile, they're susceptible to false positives, particularly during legitimate traffic spikes such as flash sales or breaking news events. Also, they need time and historical data to establish accurate baselines of normal network activity.

In practice, most ISPs employ hybrid detection models, combining signature-based engines to catch known, high-volume attacks with behavioral models that identify subtle, adaptive threats. Some devices further enhance this by using adaptive thresholds, adjusting sensitivity based on factors like time of day, location, or service type for more intelligent detection.

This dual strategy ensures networks are protected against both established threats and newer, quieter attack vectors that might bypass static defenses.

Machine Learning and AI in DDoS Detection

With the rise of advanced DDoS attacks, standard detection techniques are simply no longer enough. To address this, ISPs are increasingly leveraging machine learning (ML) and artificial intelligence (AI), which enable them to build more dynamic, predictive, and scalable systems for spotting threats.

Machine learning algorithms generally fall into two categories: supervised and unsupervised learning.

Supervised learning involves training models on labeled datasets of both normal and malicious network activity. Algorithms like decision trees, support vector machines, or neural networks learn to recognize patterns that differentiate between these two. While powerful, this approach demands extensive data preparation and becomes less effective if attackers change their tactics.

In contrast, unsupervised learning doesn't require labeled data. Instead, it analyzes network traffic to identify anomalies, outliers, or clusters. Algorithms such as autoencoders, DBSCAN, and k-means clustering can spot behavior that deviates from the norm, even if it's never been seen before. This makes unsupervised methods ideal for detecting subtle espionage or zero-day DDoS attacks.

Regardless of the approach, feature engineering is the most crucial component of any ML model. As applied to DDoS detection, common features are:

- Traffic rate: (packets per second, bits per second) to identify unusual volume.
- Source IP entropy: A sharp decline often indicates IP spoofing.
- Protocol ratios: Imbalances (e.g., in UDP vs. TCP) can signal specific attack types.
- SYN-to-ACK ratios: Extreme discrepancies may point to SYN floods.
- Flow duration and packet size variability: Deviations here can reveal abnormal traffic patterns.

Even with their promise, ML systems face challenges:

- False positives: especially during unpredictable bursts of traffic

- Adversarial learning: attackers can probe and adapt to avoid detection
- Training data quality: a lack of labeled real-world DDoS datasets can constrain effectiveness
- Operational overhead: tuning, retraining, and composition of ML pipelines at ISP scale isn't easy

A prime example of ML's utility is the use of unsupervised clustering to pinpoint low-and-slow DDoS attacks. These insidious attacks often bypass traditional threshold-based defenses, but they create discernible, dense clusters within the overall traffic landscape. ML algorithms can effectively "signal" these abnormal groupings. Another powerful application involves deep models like Recurrent Neural Networks (RNNs). By training these networks on time-series traffic data, they learn to recognize evolving patterns, allowing for the forecasting of likely attack windows. This predictive capability significantly enhances an ISP's proactive defense posture.

ML-powered detection is not a silver bullet, but when complemented with legacy solutions and human intuition, it significantly improves an ISP's likelihood of detecting and automatically responding to evolving DDoS threats.

Challenges of Malicious Traffic Detection

Perhaps the toughest challenge in malicious traffic detection, particularly in the case of DDoS detection at the ISP level, is separating the malicious traffic from regular flows. Attackers continually adapt their tactics to blend in, evade detection, and saturate defenses through stealth and quantity.

A fundamental challenge is IP spoofing, where attackers falsify the source IP address in packets to hide their origin and circumvent basic access controls. This tactic is especially prevalent in amplification attacks like DNS, NTP, or Memcached reflection, where small queries generate massive responses directed at a victim. Since the spoofed IP doesn't reveal the attacker's true location, tracing the attack back to its source becomes virtually impossible.

Another significant hurdle is differentiating legitimate flash crowds such as sudden, genuine spikes in traffic from actual DDoS attacks. For instance, a product launch, a viral tweet, or breaking news can generate traffic surges that mimic an attack. Unless carefully tuned with context, user-agent patterns, and historical baselines, behavioral detection systems are prone to falsely flagging these as threats.

An additional layer of complexity is introduced by encryption (TLS/SSL). As more internet traffic becomes encrypted, traditional payload monitoring is no longer feasible without terminating SSL sessions. ISPs, typically, cannot decrypt the traffic without forcing their users to trust its TLS certificate. Even when they have the means, they are typically unwilling to do this due to concerns about anonymity, legal implications, and efficiency. Consequently, attackers can easily bypass conventional signature-based defenses by hiding malicious content within these encrypted tunnels.

Furthermore, attackers are increasingly employing botnets and proxy networks (such as hijacked residential IPs, VPNs, and Tor) to mask their origins. These distributed, global sources effectively mimic legitimate user traffic, thereby defeating geolocation-based filtering and source reputation scoring.

These challenges demand more than passive detection; they demand adaptive solutions that bridge patterns across time, employ metadata rather than payloads, and augment technical signals with threat intelligence. As DDoS attacks grow increasingly sophisticated, effective detection increasingly relies on analyzing patterns across vast streams of seemingly normal traffic, rather than isolating individual malicious packets.

Deployment Considerations for ISP Detection Systems

Successfully implementing DDoS detection at the ISP level demands a perfect balance of accuracy, speed, and scalability. For Tier-1 and Tier-2 ISPs handling traffic volumes in the terabits per second, there's no room for inefficient or intrusive detection mechanisms.

Scalability and performance are not negotiable. Detection engines must execute in near-real time, over hundreds of interfaces, without introducing latency. This typically rules out deep packet inspection or full payload inspection at scale. ISPs, therefore, turn to flow analysis, statistical modeling, and heuristic-based flagging.

One significant design decision is between out-of-band and inline detection. Inline systems analyze traffic in-line in the transit path, allowing for real-time response such as dropping or redirecting bad flows. They do pose a risk; every failure or false alert affects live traffic. Out-of-band systems quietly analyze mirrored traffic streams for safety at the expense of responsiveness. Most ISPs use a combination of out-of-band detection and inline enforcement.

The detection system must seamlessly integrate with mitigation infrastructure. It needs to feed verdict-driven alerts and flow data directly to automated scrubbing centers, blackhole routes, or rate limiters. These mitigation platforms then act upon the detection verdicts, ensuring that detection and response layers work together flawlessly to eliminate blind spots and slow reactions.

Detection systems must also support robust logging, alerting, and SIEM pipelines. They need to collect system telemetry, NetFlow/IPFIX logs, and detection hits for forensic analysis, compliance auditing, and incident correlation. Alerts, while guaranteeing instant response to genuine threats, must be throttled with adjustable thresholds to prevent alert fatigue.

In the end, automated, modular, and fault-tolerant ISP detection implementations work best. As the core intelligence of an advanced DDoS defense strategy, these systems must continuously adapt to evolving attack methodologies, scale with network growth, and seamlessly integrate into broader security initiatives.

Chapter 6: DDoS Mitigation Strategies for ISPs

Introduction: The ISP's High-Stakes Role

Internet Service Providers (ISPs) hold a pivotal position in the online world. As the backbone of internet connectivity, they not only provide access to the users but also ensure the stability and reliability of the network. Their networks carry the information of millions of users, organizations, and platforms, positioning ISPs as a natural choke point and a top target for Distributed Denial of Service (DDoS) attacks.

Unlike application targeted attacks, ISP-level DDoS attacks have systemic consequences. A big enough or coordinated-enough volume attack can flood core routing infrastructure, bring down large sections of service, and cascade outages downstream to reliant services. Due to this, ISP-layer DDoS mitigation isn't just a straightforward service function; it's the resilience of the digital infrastructure.

Detection and mitigation are typically managed as separate operations. Detection is all about identifying unusual traffic patterns or signs of an attack as quickly as possible. Mitigation, on the other hand, is all about restricting or eliminating the impact of that attack when it's being carried out. ISPs must be prepared to carry out both at the same time under intense time constraints, attempting to balance infrastructure protection without blocking legitimate user traffic unnecessarily. The consequences are high, and the latitude for mistakes is paper-thin.

Traffic Filtering and Rate Limiting Methods

Arguably, the most immediate defense against DDoS attacks is the enforcement of traffic filtering and rate limiting across various layers of an ISP's infrastructure. These methods attempt to filter out or throttle malicious traffic prior to it reaching critical systems.

Access Control Lists (ACLs) form the core of filtering policies. ACLs are a combination of source/destination IP address, port, or protocol-based rule filters that are applied at routers to permit or deny traffic. ACLs can be applied for known threats or to block entire categories of traffic in the event of an attack. ACLs must be updated frequently in real time and handled with care to avoid collateral damage.

Flow-based filtering adds contextual richness. By analyzing such factors as packet size, rate, and flow behavior (with the help of technologies such as NetFlow or sFlow), ISPs are able to identify and block anomalous patterns that indicate a DDoS flood.

Threshold-based rate control incorporates volume-based protections. When traffic from a certain source, subnet, or protocol exceeds specific thresholds, the ISP can begin to throttle or drop traffic from those sources. This method is effective in countering brute-force volumetric attacks but less effective in countering distributed low-rate attacks.

For an ISP, filtering at its network peering edge, which is the entry point for all traffic, reduces load on downstream systems. For implementing mitigations, the closer it is to the source of traffic, the better it is in terms of efficiency. It achieves a first-pass purification, ensuring only minimally valid traffic reaches the core.

However, all filtering strategies come with their trade-offs. Over-aggressive rules can generate false positives, isolate innocent consumers and affecting service availability. Under-filtering opens the door for bad traffic to get through. Effective filters require a balance of speed, accuracy, and consideration of the costs of the operations, especially in real-time mitigation scenarios.

Null Routing / Blackholing

Null routing, or blackholing, is an active DDoS mitigation technique whereby traffic destined for a specific IP address is silently discarded at the network level. When an attack target IP is null-routed, incoming packets are forwarded to a non-existent or "black hole" location, the traffic is, in effect, taken out of the network without notifying the sender or even the receiver While the targeted IP (also known as a the victim) temporarily loses complete connectivity and is unable to access the internet, this action ensures that the ISP's network is not overwhelmed with attacker's traffic and rest of the destinations in the network continue to work properly without any network congestion. Thus, while the victim faces a loss of service and the attacker's goal of denying the service is achieved, it ensures the rest of ISP services are stable and have a minimal impact.

Remote-Triggered Black Hole (RTBH) routing enhances this technique even further by enabling routers to dynamically drop traffic based on Border Gateway Protocol (BGP) advertisements.

Within an RTBH setup, network administrators can remotely notify routers to emit null routes towards specific IPs or prefixes. This enables rapid response to dynamically evolving threats without manually configuring every router.

ISPs usually opt between automatic and selective null-routing. Selective routing is human-initiated and precise but slower to execute. Automatic null-routing initiates a null route via a pre-established threshold or detection rule, usually via a mitigation platform. More rapid in operation, it can be more susceptible to errant triggers if not implemented carefully, specifically in sophisticated multi-tenant environments.

The trade-off is harsh: saving infrastructure or keeping service accessible. Null routing is a good 'absorber' of attack traffic, but at the cost of blocking the legitimate traffic to the target IP address. For enterprise customers, this leads to disruption of important APIs, customer service applications, or DNS servers, which leads to a reputation or financial loss.

Worse still, attackers could spoof null-routing policies when a detection system in an ISP responds too rapidly. By spoofing traffic to a decoy IP address or competitor, attackers may force the ISP to null-route a legitimate service, turning the ISP's own defenses against them.

Null routing, as fast and easy as it is, must be used with restraint, preferably as a temporary measure while other stacked defenses like traffic scrubbing or filtering come into play.

Traffic Scrubbing Centers

As a final measure, when regular filtering or rate limiting is not enough, ISPs resort to traffic scrubbing centers, specifically designed facilities that seek to detect, cleanse, and forward only legitimate traffic. Scrubbing is particularly efficient for volumetric and multi-vector DDoS attacks that are meant to flood bandwidth and assault multiple protocols simultaneously.

Scrubbing centers are deployable in two primary models: inline or out-of-band.

In an inline deployment, all traffic is forced, by default, through the scrubbing infrastructure. This allows real-time filtering and inspection, but can cause latency as well as single points of failure.

In out-of-band deployments, only suspicious traffic is sent to the scrubbing center, usually through BGP redirection or GRE tunnels. This reduces operational overhead and allows clean traffic to bypass unnecessary filtering.

Then, when sent to the scrub center, traffic is scanned for known DDoS signatures, protocol abnormalities, and high-order abnormalities. Packets that pass inspection are permitted to flow to the destination IP address, while suspect or malformed packets are dropped.

Let's consider the case of a large telco under a multi-vector attack: An ISP saw a sudden spike in SYN floods and DNS amplification to one of their banking clients. The telco used BGP to redirect traffic for the client's /24 prefix via its local scrubbing facility. Traffic was decapsulated, scanned, filtered, and safely delivered through a backup tunnel, all in seconds without blackholing the IP block.

Reference link:

https://www.imperva.com/resourccs/ebooks/Playbook-The-Network-Ops-DDoS-Playbook-new.pdf)

But scrubbing centers are extremely costly and sophisticated. Scrubbing centers require high-performance gear, real-time analysis, highly available designs, and technical staff to implement dynamic policies. Misconfiguration or latency in redirection can slow down mitigation and amplify service interruptions. In addition, ISPs must balance the latency trade-offs and bandwidth charges that are incurred when tunneling and filtering large volumes of traffic.

ISP Layer Function of Content Delivery Networks (CDNs)

Content Delivery Networks (CDNs) are included in the web's defense strategy nowadays, not just for content acceleration, but also for protection against DDoS attacks. CDNs reduce the dependency on origin servers and central infrastructure by using caching at the network edge. Decentralization makes it harder for attackers to target a single point of failure and significantly improves the network's ability to withstand large-scale volumetric attacks.

For CDNs, cooperation with ISPs provides operational efficiency as well as mitigating potential issues. During a DDoS attack, traffic may be rapidly rerouted to CDN nodes that are geographically and topologically close to the attacking source. This rerouting helps localize and absorb the attack traffic before it enters the ISP's core network, saving bandwidth and reducing upstream congestion.

Some CDN services go beyond caching to offer network-level mitigation services:

- Cloudflare Magic Transit enables DDoS protection for entire blocks of IPs by using BGP advertisements to route traffic through Cloudflare's edge, worldwide.
- Akamai Prolexic accomplishes the same by filtering and redirecting traffic through its worldwide dispersed scrubbing centers.
- Fastly provides DDoS mitigation through its edge cloud platform, leveraging real-time traffic analysis and automated filtering across its globally distributed network to absorb and neutralize volumetric attacks before they reach the origin.

However, CDNs are not an elixir. As more encryption (TLS/SSL) usage increases, and traffic patterns are obfuscated, visibility and filtering are compromised. With this, attackers are able to exploit it by creating encrypted floods that can bypass trivial CDN defenses.

Ultimately, as much as CDNs cannot be employed in lieu of basic ISP mitigation infrastructure, they are a valuable addition in load distribution, concealing attack surfaces, and minimizing path to defense, especially when deployed in conjunction with other layering techniques.

Collaboration with Upstream Suppliers

During a massive DDoS attack, ISPs should not work in isolation. The overwhelming volume of traffic during high-intensity attacks typically overwhelms the capacity of individual ISPs, and collaboration with upstream ISPs, specifically Tier-1 and Tier-2 carriers, is indispensable.

ISPs may employ BGP communities and signaling to provide traffic handling instructions to be passed to upstream entities, like blackholing traffic going to certain prefixes or sending it to scrubbing infrastructure.

BGP community labels allow ISPs to notify upstream transit providers of a specific action (e.g., RTBH or traffic rerouting). These labels are mutually agreed upon in advance and interpreted automatically by routers, allowing prompt response without the need for human involvement.

ISPs also use traffic engineering techniques to spread load across more than one upstream link to prevent localized congestion. This can involve modifying BGP attributes such as MED, AS-path prepending, or local preference in order to influence route selection and balance.

Picture a 300 Gbps flood attack against one of a large ISP's customers. By asking an upstream Tier-1 provider to null route the /32 target prefix, the attack was halted before it hit the ISP's infrastructure, preserving service to the other customers.

Coordination such as this might require trust, velocity, and pre-coordinated processes, but is nonetheless one of the best ways to scale mitigation for the event of massive, geographically distributed DDoS attacks.

Inability to Deal with Adaptive and Sophisticated Attacks

Modern-day DDoS attackers are no longer relying on brute-force mechanisms. Instead of bombarding the network with one flood, attackers can blend and sequence multiple traffic types, such as SYN floods, DNS requests, and erroneous HTTP requests over varying intervals to mask detection mechanisms.

Real-time dynamic orchestration of botnets further complicates mitigation. Botnets are currently spun up in real-time using infected cloud hosts, microservices, or IoT devices. The nodes execute for brief times, quickly change IPs, and try to blend in as normal user traffic. The attacker's goal is to avoid detection long enough to induce performance degradation, add latency, or quietly use system resources.

These tactics render strict mitigation rules ineffective. IP blocklists, protocol-based filters, or rate-limit thresholds are outdated with polymorphic traffic and decentralized attack surfaces.

The only viable defense against such evolving threats is real-time, adaptive mitigation-guided by behavioral analytics, AI, and machine learning models. Such solutions can set up normal traffic behavior and identify anomalies, even without traditional indicators. They can also automatically adapt thresholds, pre-emptively prioritize suspicious flows, and correlate across telemetry layers.

With DDoS attacks becoming more sophisticated by the day, ISPs must forge new strategies from reactive filtering to predictive and dynamic response paradigms to turn mitigation into a science from an art form.

Future Directions

ISP-level DDoS mitigation is now a coordinated, multi-layered effort that demands speed, accuracy, and flexibility. This chapter touched on the prime pillars of ISP mitigation from basic methods such as ACLs and null routing, to more sophisticated techniques such as scrubbing centers, CDN integration, and upstream coordination.

The key takeaway: no single solution is enough. Instead, a strong ISP mitigation stack integrates static protections and dynamic response techniques, facilitated by trained personnel and resilient infrastructure. Real-time telemetry, dynamically adapting rules, and pre-defined escalation paths are essential to handling large-scale, adaptive DDoS attacks.

In the future, ISPs must invest in automation, observability, and global threat intelligence. Only by integrating these can they shift from reactive resistance to proactive defense.

Chapter 7: Advanced Mitigation Strategies for ISPs

Introduction: The Demand for Improved Tactics

Traditional DDoS mitigation strategies, such as traffic scrubbing centers, null routing, and offloading CDNs have been the ISPs' defense pillar. These systems, however, were born in a past era. They can be rendered powerless in the face of the modern threat landscape, where the attackers employ polymorphic tactics, decentralized botnets, and evolving attack patterns that alter in the middle of an attack. Static defenses expire faster than they can be implemented in such a scenario.

Hubs scrubbing, while robust, suffers from inducing latency and can become overwhelmed when traffic is distributed across peered networks. Null routing, while effective in emergency containment, results in service loss and is likely used as a blunt instrument. CDNs, while good at absorbing volume at the edge, offer minimal protection when the attack bypasses cacheable layers or directly attacks the origin.

ISPs are more and more likely to need intelligent routing controls, dynamic filtering tools, cross-network coordination, and legal integration. This chapter discusses these sophisticated countermeasures, beginning with an extended look at BGP Flowspec, a protocol-based solution that seeks to counter threats upstream and in step.

BGP Flowspec: Dynamic Filtering at Scale

Border Gateway Protocol (BGP) Flowspec, as defined by RFC 5575, is a major BGP extension for the propagation of traffic filtering rules to routers within a network. Unlike static ACLs or manual mitigation, Flowspec enables distributed filtering of evil traffic in real-time across multiple ingress points without hardware requirements in the center.

Essentially, BGP Flowspec achieves its goals by filtering pre-determined traffic streams on source and destination IPs, port numbers, IP protocols, and even packet lengths. For example, if an ISP identifies a UDP flood from a specific region targeting port 443, it can distribute a Flowspec filter to deny or even rate limit such traffic to all peering routers at the click of a button. This enables granular filtering and immediate reaction times without needing to reprogram every router.

Tier-1 networks and large ISPs have now started to incorporate Flowspec into their automated response playbooks. The majority of them integrate it with automatically propagating detection systems that apply rules the moment volumetric anomalies are detected. This distributed enforcement significantly reduces downstream scrubbing centers' workload and lowers collateral latency for unaffected services.

But Flowspec is not riskless. It can consume high CPU resources on routers, potentially leading to performance issues and affecting overall network efficiency. Careful management and resource allocation are essential to mitigate these risks. Ineffective filter design can lead to legitimate traffic loss, resulting in unexpected outages or poor service. It also requires careful coordination between BGP speakers to avoid routing loops or policy inconsistency. Cautions aside, BGP Flowspec remains one of the most powerful assets in the ISP arsenal for dynamic, scalable protection.

Network Peering and Upstream Filtering

Against peering partners and Tier-1 providers, pushing back upstream is one of the most effective DDoS defences at scale. ISPs usually exist as a component of a framework of interconnected networks with multiple layers. An ISP can ask upstream providers to prevent or reroute malicious traffic prior to it even touching their core infrastructure by taking advantage of these relationships.

This is usually accomplished through BGP communities, where route attributes notify the upstream peers to apply some policies. For example, a route marked with a "blackhole" community will instruct the provider to discard all traffic to that location. This is particularly useful during volumetric DDoS attacks where there isn't much scrubbing capacity or small latency budgets.

A good example of an interesting case study is a European mid-sized ISP that was targeted with a 500 Gbps UDP reflection attack. Lacking in local traffic scrubbing or absorption, the ISP collaborated with a number of Tier-1s to pre-congest markup routes using pre-configured communities. The attack traffic was null-routed at six upstream ingress points within minutes. The filter cooperation at the backbone level cut the effective size of the attack by over 80% prior to it even reaching the border of the ISP.

Another significant technique is upstream filtering of error or anomalous packets. Many large carriers allow ISPs to request filters against specific packet signatures, e.g., invalid TCP flags, fragmented payloads, or spoofed IP headers, facilitating deep packet filtering in line-rate within hardware routers.

While such upstream filtering requires trust and technical coordination, the success of volumetric attacks makes it a cornerstone of effective DDoS mitigation. As distributed and inter-regional attacks grow in number, one ISP cannot defend alone; thus, cooperative upstream mitigation is an issue of operations. 4. ISP-to-ISP Coordination and Industry Alliances

Though upstream peering protects traffic from providers, lateral collaboration between ISPs is equally critical for end-to-end DDoS security. Since attackers favor globally-disbursed botnets, defense against them means a collective effort from many network operators. This has spawned industry associations that are experts in secure routing and threat intelligence sharing.

Another well-known framework is the Information Sharing and Analysis Center (ISAC) model. ISACs specific to industry, such as the Communications ISAC, allow ISPs to exchange threat indicators, attack telemetry, and mitigation techniques confidentially. Sharing in real-time allows participants to block known vectors of attack prior to their spread.

These processes are calling for a core shift in ISP policy: from reactive single defense to proactive collective security. As attackers scale and automate, so must defenders through converged protocols, collective intelligence, and a shared dedication to making the backbone of the internet secure for all.

Law Enforcement Integration and Global Action

More than just technical prowess is frequently needed to defend against massive DDoS attacks; international cooperation and legal action are sometimes necessary. ISPs are increasingly working with law enforcement organisations including as CERTs, the FBI, Europol, and Interpol when assaults start from anonymised infrastructures, flow across borders, or pass via criminal syndicates.

In extreme cases, lawful takedown orders permit agencies to remove servers or domains under the control of botnet operators. Sinkholing forwarding botnet traffic over a controlled server is a technique to disable ongoing campaigns, gather intelligence on infected hosts, or deliver patches to infected hosts. High-profile efforts like Operation Tovar (which dismantled Gameover Zeus) indicate the impact of strong, lawful countermeasures.

But such collaboration is not without challenges. DDoS-as-a-Service websites freely advertised on the dark web operate beyond the reach of any one jurisdiction, often with bulletproof hosting. Add encryption, spoofed identities, and proxy chaining, and attributability is a vexing forensic problem.

However, by combining real-time mitigation and law enforcement cooperation, ISPs are not merely offering continuity of service, but criminal DDoS network suppression in the long term. As threats are further commercialized and politicized, this type of collaborative effort will become only more critical.

Case Studies: Patent-Based Innovations in DDoS Defense

Some of the most effective DDoS defenses have come out of actual experience that has been later patented. In fact, if you allow me to boast, I have a number of patents in botnet detection and DDoS mitigation that show how technical ingenuity can be turned into scalable security infrastructure.

One of his patents revolves around a rate-limiting algorithm through the detection of entropy. Traditional rate limiting employs flat thresholds, which are apt to miss distinguishing between organic spikes and attack floods. My innovation is measuring rates of entropy e.g., header randomness, protocol variance, or payload forms, to dynamically adjust thresholds. This allows defenses to remain permissive during natural load spikes (e.g., viral traffic) while constricting controls on the fly under DDoS.

Another patent is aimed at C2 (command-and-control) disruption of botnets on the basis of behavioral signatures. Instead of relying on detected domains or IPs, this method looks at the timing, sequence of packets, and retry logic in botnet callbacks. These properties form a fingerprint through which botnet traffic can be identified and disrupted, even when encryption or DGAs are being used.

These patents have found practical application in actual ISP deployments. At Charter Communications, for instance, entropy-based filtering was integrated within their perimeter defense stack to protect customer-facing DNS infrastructure. C2 disruption methods were integrated into anomaly detection tools and secured early warning systems during large-scale attacks.

These examples demonstrate how innovation born out of research, when scaled, can swing in favor of defenders enabling not only mitigation, but prevention and disruption of sophisticated DDoS attacks.

ISP Mitigation: Future-Facing Technologies

While DDoS attacks become more decentralized and dynamic, ISP defenses must also look beyond traditional software-defined perimeters. AI-powered threat intelligence, intent-based automation, and programmable hardware are the way of the future.

Intent-based networking (IBN) is also gaining traction at scale. IBN allows network administrators to state desired security outcomes, e.g., "block all volumetric UDP floods on port 443," and the system automatically translates those intents into configuration updates. This reduces response time under active attack by orders of magnitude and reduces operator error.

Live threat feeds, combined with machine learning-driven anomaly detection, create another degree of flexibility. By monitoring global telemetry, ISPs can also get advanced warning of emergent patterns of attack and proactively update filtering rules. A couple of premium setups even use reinforcement learning models to simulate and validate mitigation effects before deployment.

In the future, blockchain can provide decentralized solutions for proving route legitimacy or sharing threat signatures without a centralized entity. Experimental though they may be, these concepts hold potential in cases where transparency and trust are paramount.

Taken together, these technologies represent a paradigm shift away from manual, reactive defense and toward smart, automated, and predictive mitigation.

In a world where DDoS can take economies to their knees and destroy trust, strong, proactive ISP defense is a cornerstone of digital sovereignty.

Chapter 8: DDoS Detection and Prevention for Applications

Introduction to Application-Layer DDoS

Application-layer DDoS attacks are designed to exploit the functionality of the web application rather than flooding network bandwidth. They are handled at Layer 7 of the OSI stack and target particular URLs or functionalities such as login pages, searching capabilities, or baskets. Unlike volumetric or protocol-level floods that overwhelm infrastructure with traffic, application-layer DDoS attacks use apparently valid requests in an effort to consume server resources such as CPU, memory, and database connections.

What makes them most threatening is how subtle they are. A good application-layer attack can be low-volume, most often just like normal user activity, yet induce considerable performance degradation or downtime. This subtlety escapes traditional network-level countermeasures. Moreover, these kinds of attacks are more difficult to record with signature-based solutions and necessitate more sophisticated behavioral detection. Since they target logic and functionality, not bandwidth, they demand a different, more subtle technique for detection and mitigation.

Web Application Firewalls (WAFs) and How They Work

Web Application Firewall (WAF) is a significant security control that blocks, examines, and inspects HTTP/S traffic destined to and originating from a web application. Unlike traditional transport or network layer firewalls, WAFs operate at the application layer in order to protect from known and unknown threats to web vulnerabilities.

WAFs are the first line of defense against practically all OWASP Top 10 attacks except for really few of them, like SQL injection, cross-site scripting (XSS), and remote file inclusion. They can even detect malicious payloads, damaged headers, and suspicious patterns in request bodies or query strings. Most WAFs utilize rule sets or pre-baked security templates derived from typical attack vectors. They are either static or adaptive rules, adapting traffic patterns over time.

IP Reputation, CAPTCHA, and Rate Limiting

Three easy ways employed to detect and thwart application-layer DDoS attacks are IP reputation, CAPTCHA tests, and rate limiting.

IP reputation is the practice of scoring IP addresses against their past malicious behavior i.e., membership in a botnet or spammer. The security vendors maintain dynamic threat intelligence feeds that scan for these IPs in real-time. Inserting these feeds into application gateways or WAFs helps block traffic from known malicious originators before they can do any harm.

CAPTCHA (Completely Automated Public Turing test to tell Computers and Humans Apart) is another effective technique in discriminating between real users and spam bots. In that it makes the bots pay a higher cost by requiring users to solve visual challenges, click on objects, or solve simple logical puzzles, CAPTCHAs raise the attack cost of bots. Advanced types like reCAPTCHA v3 go one step further by leveraging risk scores without intruding on the user experience.

Rate limiting restricts how often a client (usually by IP or session) sends requests in a limited time frame. Static rate limits (e.g., 10 login attempts within a minute) are easy to implement but can be inflexible. Dynamic or adaptive rate limiting considers contextual signals like geolocation, user agent, and behavioral patterns, and makes the thresholds adaptive.

Combined, these controls offer a multi-layer defense against low-and-slow DDoS activity and brute-force attacks, enabling resilience at minimal cost to user experience.

Bot Detection and Mitigation

Present-day application-layer DDoS assaults are being perpetrated by increasingly advanced bots that simulate human-like behavior. IP filtering alone will no longer suffice to discover and counter these types of bot behavior; analysis and real-time intelligence are required.

Behavioral bot detection focuses on identifying habits that differentiate humans from simulated actors. Techniques include tracking mouse travel, keystroke cadence, scroll depth, and time on page. Bots will not have or have very few of these nuances, instead subverting themselves as artificial. JavaScript tests that verify DOM rendering, cookie handling, and local storage interaction also eliminate light bots.

Machine learning (ML)-based approaches take it a step ahead by taking into account user behavior on more than one axis. ML algorithms can be trained to detect anomalies in navigational behavior, interaction frequency, and session randomness. ML algorithms learn to spot novel evasion tactics used by bots over time and help in the discovery of unknown threats.

Trap endpoints and honeypots are the terms for decoy code snippets planted within web applications. One classic one is a hidden form field, which legitimate users never touch; bots, even blindly crawling HTML, might fill it in is a good sign of automation. Trap URLs, invisible links, or spoofed APIs can serve as trigger points to blacklist offending IPs.

To simplify detection and response, the majority of businesses utilize highly sophisticated bot management tools like PerimeterX, DataDome, and Cloudflare Bot Management. They provide advanced detection, accurate good bot vs. bad bot identification, and automated response in real time and high-grade global threat feeds, which reduces the necessity to create detection models from scratch.

Finally, bot mitigation is all about depth: passive clues, active scrutiny, intelligence feeds, and ongoing fine-tuning. As bots become increasingly sophisticated, so do defenses, compelling attackers to expend more in vain without unnecessarily burdening legitimate users.

Logging, Monitoring, and Anomaly Detection

Logging and monitoring are critical building blocks of DDoS protection, especially in the app space, where attacks may not trigger a traditional alert. Detailed logging gives insight into HTTP request patterns, user activity, error codes, and response times, information critical to revealing low-volume, stealthy assaults and forensic analysis.

Everything begins with centralizing and organizing logs. Tools such as ELK stack (Elasticsearch, Logstash, Kibana) can be used for web log collection and visualization. Prometheus is suited best for collecting time-series data and metrics like the rate of requests, latency, and error rate. Tools such as Grafana add both products' real-time dashboards and alerting.

Granular monitoring not only facilitates early detection but also fuels mitigation. Detection of a specific endpoint, for example, allows teams to deploy rate limits, CAPTCHA, or quarantine the service. Lacking effective observability, best defenses are blind, and logging is both shield and scalpel in application-layer DDoS protection.

DevSecOps and DDoS Prevention Integration

In modern use cases, DDoS protection must shift further from reactive patching to proactive design. It begins with the inclusion of DDoS protection in DevSecOps practices, securing early and continuously throughout the software development lifecycle.

Shift-left security involves moving defenses like WAF rules, rate limiting, and bot protection from deployment time to development time. These controls may be added as code inside CI/CD pipelines so that every build enforces consistent security checks. For instance, SQL injection blocking or request size limiting rules might be bundled up with app deployment templates and executed in staging environments.

IaC technologies such as Terraform or AWS CloudFormation enable teams to provision DDoS controls in a repeatable and scalable manner. The WAF ACLs, API Gateway throttling rules, and auto-scaling groups may be defined by a Terraform script, all in the name of maintaining all environments (dev, test, prod) in parity. This reduces human configuration errors and speeds up rollout of mitigations.

DDoS security in CI/CD pipelines can be validated using functionality and performance testing, and also tested with. Example: stress-test login spike in stage to ensure rate-limiting kicks in without cutting off user experience. Automated security gates can prevent releases from getting promoted that weaken defenses.

By incorporating DDoS resilience in code, version control, and automation practices, organizations keep risk low and agility high. It makes DDoS protection a native capability codified, auditable, and resilient with each code commit.

Auto-Scaling and Resilience Engineering

Auto-scaling is probably the most effective cloud-native method to limit DDoS floods at the application level. With traffic bursts, legitimate or illegitimate, scaling mechanisms dynamically provide surplus compute resources to absorb the load and maintain the service uptime.

Cloud infrastructure like AWS, GCP, and Azure supports dynamic web server scaling, container cluster scaling, and serverless function scaling. Autoscaling must be tuned very delicately. Thresholds cannot be too low so that in case the scale-outs are no longer needed, but not too high so that it makes the response slow, hence degrading the service quality. Buffer capacity must be set with extra headroom that traps unexpected load spikes.

Failover planning is a second pillar of resiliency. Applications that are spread across multiple availability zones or a region can be configured to send traffic over to others in case one crashes or becomes overwhelmed. Combining autoscaling with smart load balancers and health checks presents reliability under stress.

But autoscaling does come at the expense of cost. Malicious traffic can trigger aggressive scaling, and ballooning cloud bills are usually the target of an economic DDoS attack. Brokering this risk is all about marrying controls and scaling: WAFs to lower malicious traffic, rate limiting to cap abuse, and bot detection to suppress noise.

At the end of the day, resilience engineering is more about cost-friendly defense-by-design, not scale.

OWASP Top 10 Relevance to DDoS

While OWASP Top 10 has a history of focusing on data breaches and exploitation, many of its categories directly align with application-layer DDoS attacks. Identification and Authentication Failures are a common vector that bots can exhaust server resources with infinite requests to weak login endpoints. Attackers can trigger database queries, session setup, or brute-force retry, overwhelming server backends.

Lack of Sufficient Logging and Monitoring blinds organizations to low-and-slow attacks. Without logging, abnormal spikes in failed logins or malformed requests are not visible until performance is impacted or users are locked out.

Lastly, poor application design keeps the door open to not only information theft but also to resource depletion. Securing applications from DDoS begins with plugging these architectural holes.

Case Study: Application-Layer DDoS Attack and Recovery

Early in 2023, a fintech company went months with service downtime due to an application-layer DDoS attack on its login API endpoint. The attackers flooded the endpoint with what appeared to be normal requests, thousands per second, to make the app establish sessions, read from databases, and call downstream services. The result: server CPU saturation, login timeouts for customers, and sluggishness in the mobile app.

Early indication was through a spike of authentication failures being logged in Kibana. The solution was to employ emergency rate limiting, add a CAPTCHA on the logon page, and block high-risk IP blocks by using threat intelligence.

Post-breach analysis revealed the API to lack rate limiting and session caching, and to be non-optimized for its database queries. Architectural changes included the introduction of WAF rules, load-balancing login processing into a single microservice, and the addition of bot detection software.

Summary and Strategic Takeaways

Application-layer DDoS attacks are subtle yet very powerful. Defense against them requires a defense-in-depth approach applying WAFs, rate limiting, behavioral bot blocking, and fault tolerance. Adding DevSecOps upfront, in conjunction with continuous monitoring, keeps threats at bay before they arise.

Preventive controls (like CAPTCHA and IP reputation) and reactive controls (like auto-scaling and failover) are required. No single tool can offer sufficient protection.

Lastly, protecting the application layer is not only a matter of security because it's a matter of business continuity. And whereas threats become more complex, so must our defenses.

Chapter 9: Advanced Mitigation Strategies and New Trends

Introduction: Why Advanced Mitigation is Important

In the previous chapters, we went over the building blocks of DDoS defense: firewalls, rate limiting, blackholing, and even ISP-level scrubbing. These classic methods are the backbone of defense schemes and still serve as critical first lines of defense. The online battlefront has changed, though. Today's attackers use botnets that run across millions of devices, exploit novel protocols such as QUIC, and hide within encrypted traffic. Static defenses, which were once adequate, are now increasingly overrun, bypassed, and even used as an attack vector.

This fact compels enterprises and service providers to consider beyond reactive mitigation. Yesterday's attack patterns can be halted by traditional tools, but they usually fail against adaptive, stealthy, and massive campaigns trying to fit into legitimate traffic.

Artificial intelligence and machine learning are increasingly being integrated into defense systems, providing dynamic detection and near real-time reaction to emerging threats. Threat intelligence information sharing has also become imperative, ensuring that the shared experiences of attacks fortify the entire ecosystem. And as we look ahead, sophisticated strategies grounded in innovation and collaboration are no longer a choice; they are a matter of survival within a threat environment that will not stand still.

Machine Learning and AI in DDoS Protection

Machine learning and artificial intelligence have rapidly become at the heart of contemporary DDoS protection, thanks to their capability to analyze massive amounts of traffic data and identify patterns that are invisible to human operators or fixed systems. Fundamentally, ML algorithms are able to process traffic flows in real time, set baselines of normal behavior, and detect anomalies that indicate an imminent or in-progress attack. In contrast to signature-based systems, which are based on preconceived rules, ML-based systems adapt as the traffic adapts, learning new attack approaches without the need for updates.

One of the greatest strengths of ML is its ability to separate malicious traffic from normal spikes in demand. For instance, an online retailer on Black Friday will have traffic surges that seem superficially very much like a DDoS flood. An adaptive ML system will be able to differentiate because it can look at deeper behavioral features, session durations, request diversity, geographic dispersal, and avoid false alarms while continuing to detect real attacks.

Some of the key applications are traffic baselining, wherein ML models establish "normal" patterns for specific times of day or business cycles; predictive modeling, enabling defenders to foretell attack escalation before services crash; and automated mitigation, wherein countermeasures like rate limiting, rerouting, or scrubbing occur without having to wait for human response.

However, AI-based defense has its problems given AI based generative solutions are fundamentally non-deterministic in nature.

It cannot provide absolute guarantees when posed with complex challenges which is why relying solely on AI can be a recipe for disaster. False positives are still a problem since mistakenly marking legitimate users can hurt customer confidence. Attackers are now testing out adversarial AI, designing traffic that misleads or evades detection algorithms. Finally, the processing overhead of real-time inspection demands solid infrastructure investment. AI can be used to augment and extend existing capabilities but not as a way to completely replace the traditional defense systems and human oversight.

In spite of such challenges, actual cloud AI-based platforms like those embedded in top cloud DDoS protection solutions are already demonstrating their worth. Such platforms have already defeated multi-terabit assaults by modifying filtering methods dynamically within seconds. The path is evident: AI and ML are not merely voluntary bells and whistles but integral support columns of a contemporary, robust DDoS defense system.

Threat Intelligence as Proactive Defense

Speed is the essence of DDoS defense. Before an attack saturates infrastructure, mitigation is expensive and intrusive. This is where threat intelligence comes into play. Common intelligence feeds like IP reputation lists, botnet activity feeds, and exploit databases enable defenders to filter out known bad sources before they reach the target. These feeds are updated constantly from worldwide monitoring systems that observe botnet behavior, malware spread, and anomalous traffic patterns.

Today's Threat Intelligence Platforms (TIPs) bring this data into operational processes, using automation to ingest, correlate, and apply intelligence. A TIP, for instance, can add context to raw network traffic: is this IP associated with a variant of Mirai, has it engaged in reflection attacks, or is it part of a doubtful autonomous system? Layering such intelligence enables defenders to respond more quickly and accurately, with less collateral damage.

Collaboration strengthens this value. When enterprises, ISPs, and governments engage in intelligence-sharing communities, they create a shared defense. An attack witnessed in one area can be protected against globally in hours, blocking cascading effects. Programs such as MISP (Malware Information Sharing Platform) and national CERT programs are the best examples of this collaborative model.

An example: during coordinated DDoS attacks against financial institutions, cross-border intelligence sharing allowed banks to blacklist the malicious IPs in a matter of minutes. Rather than experiencing days of downtime, services were quickly restored, and customer confidence was maintained. This shows how proactive intelligence is not merely defense but also keeping resilience and continuity intact.

DDoS Signaling and Collaborative Defense

As DDoS attacks become larger in size, it's impossible for anyone organization to combat them by itself. Even the most hardened businesses depend on upstream providers and ISPs to filter and absorb malicious traffic. To automate this cooperation, the industry has created signaling mechanisms to enable networks to exchange attack data in real-time.

One of the central innovations is the DDoS Open Threat Signaling (DOTS) protocol, which the IETF standardized. DOTS allows victims and mitigation providers to have a shared language to communicate with. Rather than waiting for human telephone calls or sticky tickets, a DOTS client can automatically alert a scrubbing provider that it is experiencing an attack, identify the traffic type involved, and ask for mitigation immediately.

The advantage is obvious: quicker response times, fewer human mistakes, and defensible defense on a scalable basis across numerous networks. Picture a worldwide attack where enterprises, ISPs, and cloud services all send DOTS signals to each other, traffic can be redirected and cleaned en masse before it ever hits the victim.

Forward-looking researchers see autonomous collaborative defense networks in the future, where AI-based systems share threat information and mitigation instructions without human agency. In such a future, DDoS defense would be a digital immune system, distributed, adaptive, and learning from every attack.

DDoS Information Sharing

The DDoS Information Sharing (DIS) Project deserves an honorary mention in this chapter as a pioneering effort in multi-lateral cybersecurity collaboration. This project was a joint initiative between leading Internet Service Providers (ISPs), facilitated through the multi-lateral communication channels of the M3AAWG (Messaging, Malware and Mobile Anti-Abuse Working Group) and provided with technical development and infrastructure support by CableLabs, a neutral non-profit organization which focuses on research and development around new cable and internet technologies. This collaborative working group now includes DDoS practitioners from various ISPs around the world.

The DIS project marked a first-of-its-kind initiative by establishing a trusted, central platform where competitors could exchange critical attack data:

- Source IP Sharing: The system's primary innovation was the ability for participating ISPs to share information about the source IP addresses of malicious traffic (devices launching attacks, often compromised IoT devices or bots).
- Privacy Preservation: This sharing was achieved while guarding the privacy of their respective subscribers by masking the victim IPs and other sensitive information.
- Centralized Intelligence: The data is funneled into a central database, often utilizing the CRITS (Collaborative Research Into Threats) platform and open-source tools developed by CableLabs, which acts as a hub for anti-abuse groups and cybersecurity professionals.
- Impact: By identifying and reporting persistent threat sources, the project helped streamline mitigation processes

across the industry, increasing the difficulty for malicious actors to make devastating large-scale attacks.

This project underscores the commitment within the ISP community to move beyond individual defenses and establish a collaborative security posture against the growing threat of distributed attacks. I am proud to have been a part of this project during my tenure at Charter Communications.

New Attack Vectors

DDoS attacks are coming in many forms beyond naive traffic floods, employing new technologies and protocols in ways that test old-fashioned defenses. One of the most significant developments is the emergence of QUIC-based attacks. Google-designed QUIC, adopted extensively in HTTP/3, enhances web performance by merging transport and security layers. Unfortunately, its encrypted-by-default nature and connection resumption capabilities make it more difficult for defenders to analyze or filter malicious traffic. Attackers take advantage of this by concealing floods inside QUIC packets, rendering classic mitigation tools blind.

Meanwhile, botnets of the Internet of Things keep increasing the size of DDoS attacks. Billions of inadequately protected devices, everything from cameras to routers and even smart refrigerators, are readily hijacked into huge legions. Their variety makes it hard to defend against, since their traffic is indistinguishable from regular consumer traffic to millions of different geographical areas.

Attackers are also getting creative with reflection and amplification attacks, going beyond the usual vectors of DNS and NTP. New services, such as leaked gaming servers or IoT protocols, are being exploited to reflect traffic at amplification factors higher than older attacks. These new amplifiers make attack power higher while keeping the attacker's footprint low.

In the meantime, application-layer stealth attacks pose another devious threat. Rather than clogging bandwidth, they focus on using low-traffic but thoughtfully formulated requests to drain server resources. As an example, requiring thousands of incomplete HTTP requests can occupy web servers without triggering classical traffic alert levels.

For the defenders, one thing only can be said about such trends: DDoS mitigation has to keep evolving. Strategies have to prepare for attacks embedded in novel protocols, encrypted streams, or low-rate stealth traffic. Static defense is not enough; the defenders need to adopt adaptive detection, sharing of intelligence, and more in-depth inspection techniques to keep abreast of a fast-evolving battlefield.

Encryption and the Challenge of TLS/SSL

Encryption has become the default for internet traffic. Although this is a win for security, it poses a critical challenge to DDoS defense: encrypted traffic cannot be easily inspected. Attackers take advantage of this blind spot, sending floods of HTTPS requests that are legitimate-looking but brute servers and tie up enormous CPU cycles to decrypt.

The balance here is obvious: privacy and visibility have to be traded off. Decrypting traffic to examine it threatens to reveal sensitive information, and not decrypting leaves defenses in the dark. Two ways to mitigate are SSL offloading, in which decryption is performed at specialized hardware or load balancers and then passes on traffic analysis before it gets to critical applications, and TLS fingerprinting, in which metadata (for example, cipher suites, handshake patterns, or certificate anomalies) is inspected without decrypting payloads, and providing useful detection signals.

New solutions revolve around encrypted traffic analytics (ETA), applying AI and statistical models to deduce malicious activity from flow metrics such as packet size, timing, and session duration without the need for complete decryption. This offers a middle ground between security and privacy.

Blockchain and Decentralized Defense

Classic DDoS mitigation tends to rely on centralized scrubbing centers or service providers, but these strategies risk becoming bottlenecks or single points of failure. The concept of decentralized DDoS mitigation attempts to turn this paradigm upside down. By spreading mitigation capabilities across a broad base of participants, defenders can water down the effect of gigantic floods and prevent overdependence upon a handful of providers.

Several pilot studies and research projects have tried using blockchain-based "decentralized scrubbing." In these systems, overflow traffic is transferred to volunteer or incentivized nodes that scrub and send back only valid requests, much like content delivery networks (CDNs), but in a more democratized fashion.

Despite this, adoption is confronted with challenges. Blockchain-based defense mechanisms may be challenged with latency, scalability, and power use, which are vital in time-critical DDoS attacks. Furthermore, international involvement demands legal and operational synchronization that proves challenging to enforce. Decentralized defense is promising but more of an experimental edge than an operational norm.

Sophisticated ISP-Level Strategies

ISPs hold a special place in the DDoS ecosystem: they have control over the pipes over which the attacks travel. Sophisticated mitigation tactics at this point are essential to dampening the size of attacks prior to their arrival at enterprises.

One of the potent weapons available is BGP Flowspec, which allows ISPs to distribute traffic-filtering rules throughout their networks near real-time. Malicious traffic patterns, e.g., specific port floods or malformed packets, can be discarded at multiple points of entry simultaneously, containing the attack at scale, using Flowspec.

Upstream peering and filtering move this further by locating the defense nearer to the source of an attack. Rather than taking floods at the victim's ISP, traffic can be scrubbed at upstream providers or peering exchanges, cutting down on downstream congestion.

Inter-ISP coordination is also becoming mandatory. By having scrubbing centers shared and signaling protocols such as DOTS, ISPs are able to share attack intelligence and divide up mitigation efforts across networks and borders.

Organizational Preparation and Awareness

Whereas technology constitutes the foundation of DDoS protection, the human factor is equally vital. Organizations need to see their teams properly equipped to detect and respond to attacks rapidly, keeping both technical and business impact to a minimum. This starts with awareness initiatives that make employees aware of the nature of DDoS threats and the part they play in threat escalation or containment.

Simulation exercises and red-teaming training allow valuable practice where teams can practice their responses in realistic settings. These exercises are used to discover process weaknesses, attempt communication links, and enforce cross-team collaboration.

Attackers are also using psychology by means of socially engineered DDoS situations, like false alarms or deceptive warnings meant to create panic or mislead defenders. Occasionally, DDoS attacks are used as a strategic diversion, which diverts attention while malware or ransomware is enacted in tandem. Getting staff ready to identify and counter these tactics is key to comprehensive resilience.

Case Studies of Advanced Attack and Reaction

- Case 1: Global attack enabled by synchronised IoT. DNS providers were subjected to a protracted, multi-terabit barrage orchestrated by a botnet comprising millions of compromised IoT devices. Large platforms were inaccessible due to the magnitude, which simultaneously overpowered several regions. Only cross-ISP coordination and emergency rerouting were able to mitigate the issue, underscoring the need for global coordination.

- Case 2: QUIC-based DDoS attacks against financial institutions. Attackers exploited QUIC's encrypted traffic streams to cause outages at a multinational bank. The bank had to separate hostile traffic from legitimate traffic using TLS fingerprinting and AI-powered analysis because traditional firewalls were unable to detect the attack.

The Road Ahead

The nature of DDoS defense mirrors a distinct movement away from static, reactive solutions to adaptive, intelligence-led strategies. No more can companies depend on rate limiting and blackholing alone; survival requires agility, automation, and forethought. Cooperation between governments, ISPs, enterprises, and worldwide intelligence networks will be the measure of the power of tomorrow's defenses. Innovation in even decentralized models, encrypted traffic analysis, and AI will continue to shape the landscape. On the horizon, the era of quantum and AI-powered cyber war will create new uncertainties, rendering preparedness an elusive target. The future of defense is in collective strength and the constant pursuit of innovation.

Chapter 10: Application Resilient Architecture Design

Introduction: Why Resilience Matters

Information security can describe the capability of an application to resist disruptions, be they from attackers, technical failure, or unexpected usage bursts, without losing key services as resilience. Continuity takes priority with resilience, making sure fundamental operations stay online and available even under attack, unlike mere security, which is designed to block intrusions.

Crisis conditions are generally employed to differentiate between robust and brittle architectures. A brittle system might carry normal traffic but collapses when resources become overloaded, leading to cascading failures that take down the target application along with supporting services.

Minutes of downtime could cost banks millions of dollars. Bad publicity, lost confidence, and failed transactions are all issues for e-commerce sites. One outage can cause regulatory breaches, fines, and damage to reputation for businesses selling in regulated industries. Downtime equals lost opportunity and reputation in the digital-first economy.

Scalability and Redundancy Principles

Redundancy and scalability are two complementary factors that constitute the building blocks of resilient architecture. Together, they help applications grow to accommodate increasing demand without compromising reliable delivery.

Scalability refers to the ability to cope with growth. PowerCPU, memory, or storage is appended vertically to one server. While effective to an extent, vertical scaling has constraints and creates single points of failure. Horizontal scaling, however, adds more servers or instances and distributes the load across multiple nodes. Cloud computing has added to this concept by bringing in elasticity, wherein resources scale up or down in real time based on demand.

Redundancy complements scalability in ensuring that duplicate resources can step in when the originals fail. The N+1 approach, for instance, ensures that there is always at least one spare instance. Improved designs utilize active-active configurations where several nodes load-balance in parallel, yielding high availability. Or active-passive ones detect standby resources that only become active upon failure. All the models provide outage insurance, but active-active will give more performance during an attack.

The redundancy and scalability have the ability to keep off DDoS attacks effectively, as seen in the following real-world scenario: an e-commerce giant globally faced a 300 Gbps volumetric attack that would have knocked off less robust systems. What its elastic infrastructure did was to buffer the spike by dynamically adding servers in multiple regions. Traffic was directed through redundant load balancers, keeping customers served without a hitch anywhere in the world. The incident showed that resilience is not theoretical and can be the difference between collapse and continuity.

Distributed Systems and Microservices

Decentralization is among the most effective approaches to building resilience. With a monolithic structure, the loss of any one database, application logic, or network failure can bring down the entire system. Distributed systems, however, distribute workloads among several nodes and split the loads so that failures are localized within the domains rather than spreading across the entire system.

But microservices have their own set of problems. Too many services lead to microservice sprawl and make dependencies complex to manage. Inter-service communication adds latency, which becomes a bottleneck if one microservice is critical to multiple workflows. Without good design, a seemingly resilient system can create new vulnerabilities.

It is here that orchestration platforms like Kubernetes become relevant. Kubernetes ensures that deployment, scaling, and failover of services are automated so that microservices running in containers can fail over transparently.

Traffic Management and Load Balancing

For even the most dispersed and scalable infrastructures to function efficiently under pressure, intelligent traffic management is necessary. By distributing incoming requests evenly among the available resources, load balancing guarantees that no node is ever overloaded. Resilience is directly impacted by algorithm selection. In order to lower the risk of overload, round robin sends traffic to the server with the fewest active sessions and balances requests. By allowing traffic to be redirected to servers with greater capacity, weighted balancing adds flexibility and heterogeneity.

In addition to simple distribution, geo-load balancing offers geographical redundancy. By directing users to the nearest or most healthy data center, geo-load balancing optimizes latency and redundancy. Network traffic can be rerouted automatically to other geos if one geo becomes unreachable, it is a localized DDoS attack, or infrastructure outage.

At the DNS level, more advanced techniques like Anycast routing and Global Server Load Balancing (GSLB) offer redundancy on top of that. Not only does it accelerate user access, but it also distributes malicious traffic worldwide, diluting the impact of DDoS floods. GSLB takes this further by weighing server health and location before routing requests.

Lastly, load balancing is not only an efficiency mechanism but also a security strategy. By spreading valid and malicious traffic in an intelligent manner, it prevents bottlenecks, diffuses attack pressure, and gives users instant service continuity even if the infrastructure gets targeted.

Caching and Content Delivery Networks

Caching is quite possibly the simplest but most powerful mechanism of improving application resiliency. By keeping data accessed in the recent past in a temporary yet readily available space, caches reduce the burden on backend systems and split bursts of traffic. At the database level, the answers to queries can be cached to avoid redundant execution of expensive operations. Object caches, with systems like Redis or Memcached, improve access to static or semi-static objects like user sessions or product catalogs. Fragment caching or full-page caching at the application level ensures that even dynamic web pages can return precomputed results under a heavily loaded condition.

Pinging caching to the network edge, CDNs are the first line of defense against DDoS attacks. CDNs mirror content across edge servers worldwide, distributed in population, ensuring requests are fulfilled locally. Volumetric attacks that can overload a single data center are instead distributed across hundreds of CDN nodes.

Real-world providers such as Cloudflare, Akamai and Fastly have built their reputations following this edge defense paradigm. Their infrastructures can scale up to absorb hundreds of terabits per second in attacks, offering protection that single organizations cannot achieve by themselves.

An example of a fintech startup presents a revealing case study. When smacked with incessant Layer 7 HTTP floods aimed at exhausting application resources, the company added Cloudflare to its infrastructure. The CDN cached commonly-used responses at the edge and filtered out malicious traffic before it reached the origin. Outcome: uninterrupted service amidst weeks of attempts at disruption, with the startup customers never having an inkling that an attack was taking place.

Defense in Depth for Applications

Strong architectures are not based on a single protection but on a sequence of layers of security commonly known as defense in depth. This pattern ensures that if one of the protective measures is bypassed, other layers are still there to safeguard the application.

On the periphery of deployment, Web Application Firewalls (WAFs) act as sentinels, preventing malicious requests such as SQL injection or HTTP floods. API gateways complement WAFs by controlling access to backend services, authenticating, and enacting throttling policies to reduce abuse.

The Zero Trust paradigm strengthens these layers by assuming that no request, either internal or external, should ever be trusted initially. Every interaction is authenticated, authorized, and encrypted, significantly reducing the potential for attackers to take advantage of poor internal trust models.

The strength of defense in depth is that it is redundant. A DDoS attacker will be able to flood one protection, but it is the cascading controls that continue to operate the application. If a WAF fails to catch a hidden HTTP flood, rate limiting on the API gateway can still throttle the requests. Microsegmentation also ensures that even when one microservice is breached, the attack does not spread across the system.

By designing applications with multiple, redundant defense layers, organizations transform what would otherwise be single points of failure into hardened perimeters, providing architectures that are resilient to long-term, multi-vector attacks.

Architectural Patterns for Applications that Defend Against DDoS

Aside from overall principles like redundancy and scalability, reliable systems will utilize specific architectural forms that are designed to withstand massive DDoS assaults and system collapse. These styles provide systematic approaches to spreading risk, containing failure, and delivering graceful degradation.

Among the most powerful is Anycast Routing, where multiple servers globally share the same IP address. Requests would naturally be directed to the nearest or most accessible server, which distributes both valid and evil traffic geographically.

Multi-region deployment extends resilience even further by executing applications across several independent geographic areas. When a single region crashes from an attack, loss of power, or natural disaster traffic is routed automatically to other regions. Disaster recovery zones provide this approach as backups with data and infrastructure synchronized.

At the service level, circuit breaker patterns protect against cascading failures. If a microservice hangs, the circuit breaker halts requests to it briefly, so upline systems are not dragged down with it. Bulkhead isolation also isolates services, so a failing microservice cannot monopolize all system resources. Taken together, these patterns transform what might be catastrophic failures into contained disruptions.

Resilience must be demonstrated; it cannot be theoretical. Enter chaos engineering. By deliberately breaking things in orchestrated failures in production environments, organizations verify whether their systems behave as they are expected to under pressure.

Infrastructure Resilience and Geo-Distribution

Building reliable applications requires as reliable an infrastructure. Two approaches dominate in existing strategies: multi-cloud and hybrid-cloud deployment. Multi-cloud spreads workloads between multiple providers (e.g., AWS, Azure, GCP), distributing risk away from a single vendor and keeping operations going if an individual provider is subjected to outages. Hybrid cloud converges public cloud scale with private cloud or on-premises control, delivering compliance flexibility in industries with high compliance levels. They both reduce concentration risk at the expense of greater architectural complexity.

In these deployments, failover provides unbroken continuity. Hot standby environments have completely active duplicate systems ready to take over at a moment. Warm standby incorporates partially active infrastructure held in reserve, requiring minimal bootstrapping to get underway. Cold standby employs idle infrastructure that is brought online only on failurelower expense but longer recovery. The choice relies upon cost versus recovery time targets (RTO).

Geo-distribution also increases resilience by placing infrastructure in multiple regions. This ensures that latency to users is minimized while there is redundancy between continents. An example is a DDoS attack on servers in Europe, which can be countered locally and traffic forwarded to North America or Asia. Such a distribution also addresses data residency, ensuring compliance with laws.

Banking is an excellent case in point here. Financial institutions demand multi-region resiliency and recovery procedures to be extensively tested. Banks usually have multiple active data centers with hard failover controls so that critical financial services, such as ATMs and electronic payments, remain online even in the event of colossal outages or cyber-attacks.

By investing in geo-distribution and failover solutions, organizations make infrastructure a disruption-proof shield that offers a safety net for availability, compliance, and performance.

Stress Testing and Simulation Drills

No matter how superb the architecture of a design is, resilience must be subjected to test under stress. This is where simulation drills and stress testing are essential. Through the simulation of actual attack scenarios, organizations can expose weaknesses that theoretical planning generally misses.

A useful technique is red teaming, where professional teams simulate adversarial DDoS attacks against an organization's infrastructure. Through these simulations, how defenses actually function and where playbooks vs. response splits are revealed. Red team operations are complemented by automated load testing tools such as Apache JMeter, Locust, and k6, which initiate controlled bursts of traffic to evaluate system performance against overload scenarios.

But testing has to extend beyond whether defenses work. Equally critical is mocking out failover and rollback. If an overwhelmed primary data center, can traffic fail over into another region? If a mitigation rule drops good traffic, can it be rolled back before there is extended downtime? Such scenarios often mark the boundary between graceful degradation and crash.

The Economics of Resilient Design

Constructing solid architectures is as much a matter of fiscal necessity as a technological one. Every choice to scale, replicate, or implement advanced defenses comes with a cost so does downtime. Downtime for an hour can run e-commerce sites millions in lost revenue, and financial institutions, regulatory fines, and reputational damage far greater than tangible losses of cash.

A cost-benefit analysis will typically reveal that the cost of resilience is cheap compared to the cost of disruption. For example, investing in additional load balancers or subscribing to a high-end CDN service may result in monthly recurring costs, but will delay losses of an order of magnitude higher in the event of a large-scale DDoS attack.

Cloud platforms formalize this principle with elastic cost structures. Unlike fixed infrastructure, where they must over-provision redundant capacity at a high upfront cost, cloud infrastructure enables them to pay for only what they use. Elastic scale enables firms to dynamically ingest attack traffic at a cost correlated to usage.

Over time, forward-thinking resilience investments have high ROI. Not only do they recover downtime losses, but they also create customer trust, protect brand reputation, and ensure regulatory compliance.

Last but not least, resilience must be framed as an operational expense in order to do business, not an elective luxury. Companies that have this mentality don't consider resilience overhead, but a competitive value that propels long-term growth.

Constructing for the Inevitable

Resilience is not something to check off on a list, but something that has to be an ongoing process. Systems that seem strong now can fail later as attackers adapt their techniques, infrastructure becomes more sophisticated, and user expectations become more demanding. Real resilience doesn't come from creating flawless defenses, but from growing architectures and cultures that learn, bounce back, and get stronger when disrupted.

The future is headed towards an AI-driven self-healing architecture that detects anomalies, segments compromised services, and initiates recovery without intervention. These technologies will shift resilience away from reactive defense and toward proactive, automated protection.

But no technology alone guarantees survival. Resilience must be a shared responsibility between developers, operations teams, and business leaders. All are involved in creating redundancy, practicing response, and making sense of investment.

Chapter 11: Incident Response and Recovery for DDoS Attacks

Introduction: When the Storm Hits

It begins as any other business day. An online platform experiences an unexpected surge of visitors thousands per second. Initially, the ops team is ecstatic, thinking it's a flash sale victory. A minute later, the bash becomes pandemonium. Pages freeze, transactions crash, and support lines are overwhelmed with furious customers. Within less than a decade, revenue comes to a standstill, systems are clogged, and hysteria grips departments.

Even the safest infrastructure can collapse when its defense is not in sync. For an attacker, the biggest advantage of a DDoS attack is not the traffic, but the disarray. Firewalls, servers, and even humans become out of sync when pressure is at its highest. This chapter takes that chaos and turns it into clarity. It walks you through the Incident Response and Recovery process, the art of taking a digital disaster and turning it into a strategic comeback. Because DDoS defense isn't solely about packet blocking, it's about coordinating people, processes, and technology in harmony when the storm comes.

Knowing the DDoS Incident Response Lifecycle

Every resilient business address DDoS defense as not a response, but rather a readiness continuum. The NIST Incident Response Lifecycle, once modified to fit DDoS, provides a predictable journey through the storm:

- Preparation – Setting up detection tools, playbooks, escalation routes, and coordination with partners.
- Detection & Analysis – Identification of anomalies, categorization of attack vectors, and ensuring the event is malicious, not organic.
- Containment, Eradication, and Recovery – Isolating impacted systems, stemming the current flood, bringing back normalcy, and confirming stability.
- Post-Incident Activities – Analysis of the event, enhancing defenses, and codifying lessons learned.

What makes DDoS unique compared to other incidents is its speed, intensity, and visibility. Breaches unfold quietly; DDoS attacks scream. They're public, immediate, and often impact business reputation within minutes.

Incident response maturity matures through phases. Small startups might depend on manual mitigation, developers frantically blocking IPs. Mature ISPs or enterprises, by contrast, use automated orchestration, routing malicious traffic to scrubbing centers, activating pre-approved vendors, and publishing coordinated stakeholder notifications in minutes.

This lifecycle turns firefighting into foresight, enabling defenders to see ahead, respond, and come out stronger after each attack.

Preparation Phase: Building the War Chest

The greatest DDoS defense doesn't start when the attack begins; it starts in the calm before the storm. Preparation is the foundation of incident response, making uncertainty actionable. It guarantees that when the first malicious packet reaches you, your team already has a plan, knows who to call, and which levers to pull.

- Playbook Design:

Each second matters in the course of a DDoS attack. A well-crafted, pre-established incident response playbook dispels uncertainty. It defines roles, escalation procedures, and SOPs for all circumstances volumetric floods, application-layer slow attacks, or multi-vector attacks. Each playbook must trace escalation paths from the SOC to management and provide technical and executive alignment. Scenario-driven decision trees (e.g., when to initiate scrubbing center activation) turn panic into procedure.

- Tools and Infrastructure:

Your monitoring environment is the response nervous system. Technologies such as NetFlow, ELK Stack, and Grafana dashboards present real-time traffic health in a visualized manner. Built-in alerting via SIEM and SOC processes ensures that certain anomalies are recognized in real time. Advanced teams implement automated defenses via BGP Flowspec rules or API-based route rerouting to mitigation providers, reducing manual lag.

The response group needs to have Security Operations, Network Engineers, DevOps, Legal, and PR. Periodic simulation exercises from Red Team attacks to Purple Team collaboration verify readiness under duress. These exercises bring up communication disparities ahead of actual crises.

- Vendor & ISP Collaboration:

Negotiate DDoS mitigation SLAs with ISPs and third-party defenders prior to an attack. Joint visibility and pre-agreed escalation pathways save critical time.

- Business Continuity Planning (BCP):

Prepare failover architecture, geo-distributed backups, cloud redundancy, and load balancing. Ensure mission-critical services can pivot seamlessly under fire.

Ultimately, DDoS resilience starts long before the first packet hits your servers. It starts with planning, partnerships, and practice.

Detection and Analysis: Knowing When You're Under Siege

The initial challenge in any DDoS attack is recognizing that an attack has actually started. Spikes in traffic can be caused by viral marketing or a breaking news story as easily as by malicious activity. The secret is disciplined detection and analysis, separating popularity from peril.

Key Detection Techniques:

- Anomaly Detection: Create traffic baselines and look for anomalies, unusual spikes in connection requests, DNS queries, or bandwidth use.
- Signature-Based Identification: Compare incoming patterns against recognized botnet activity or packet payloads based on threat intelligence databases.
- Behavioral Analytics: Utilize AI and ML patterns that mark anomalies such as unusual SYN flood rates, repeated request patterns, or high connection churn rates.
- External Threat Intelligence Correlation: Intersect network events with Indicators of Compromise (IoCs) from worldwide threat feeds and info-sharing blocs.

Common Challenges:

- False Positives: Marketing events or flash sales mimic attack patterns.
- Encryption Barriers: An increase in TLS/SSL traffic restricts packet inspection depth.
- Human-Mimicking Bots: Sophisticated DDoS attacks mimic real user activity, which is more difficult to identify.

Recommended Practices:

Implement layered visibility aggregate network flow data, endpoint logs, and application metrics for end-to-end analysis. Provide real-time dashboards with dynamically updating thresholds that automatically adjust for traffic trends. Include early-warning alerts that immediately activate escalation workflows.

In DDoS battles, detection isn't a technological achievement; it's the turning point when bewilderment yields to mastery.

Containment: Holding the Line

After a DDoS attack is validated, the focus shifts immediately from identification to containment to isolate and nullify the threat before it brings down vital services. Containment is not so much about perfection as it is about stabilization under stress. The aim is straightforward: keep vital systems running while diminishing the effect of the attack.

- Network Layer:

At this root level, rapid defensive reactions are the difference between a fleeting pause and a complete blackout. Network teams use rate limiting, blackholing, or sinkholing to send or drop malicious packets. Sophisticated defenders use BGP Flowspec to dynamically filter attack patterns at the routing level or initiate upstream filtering with ISPs, halting volumetric floods before they hit internal links.

- Transport Layer:

In these, the objective is to make connection handling more robust. SYN cookie enforcement techniques help counter SYN floods, while TCP connection limits eliminate resource exhaustion. Tweaking timeouts and protocol configuration optimization reduces the system's vulnerability to half-open connections.

- Application Layer:

DDoS attacks targeting HTTP, APIs, or authentication endpoints require rapid tuning. WAF (Web Application Firewall) rules can be adjusted to block malicious headers or repetitive payloads. Deploy CAPTCHA challenges, geo-blocking, or token-based validations to separate legitimate users from bots. Platforms like AWS Shield and Cloudflare's "I'm Under Attack" mode automate many of these steps, an instant barrier of layered verification without manual effort.

- Operational Coordination:

Containment is communication-intensive. Create a single "War Room" (physical or virtual) that brings NOC, SOC, DevOps, and vendor teams together in real time. Define unambiguous escalation and decision-making authority, such as:

- When to activate scrubbing centers.
- When to segregate or throttle non-mission-critical services (e.g., turning off search or login throttling).

- Containment purchases time, the valuable window during which to counterattack wisely and restore order without disintegration.

Eradication and Recovery: Bringing Systems Back to Life

Once the flood starts to recede, focus shifts to eradication and recovery, the intentional, systematic procedure of cleaning up the environment and going back to normal business.

- Eradication:

Residual imprints of the attack may remain, malicious requests trapped in caches, queues, or load balancers may keep taxing resources long after the peak traffic rush abates. Removing these imprints is priority number one. Then, patch or reconfigure any vulnerability that was taken advantage of, like open APIs or overly open firewall policies. A complete infrastructure sweep comes next, making sure that the DDoS wasn't a cover story for a more pervasive compromise, like malware implantation or credential exfiltration.

- Recovery:

Recovery is a staged process, not a flip of the switch. Begin with progressive traffic restoration, returning normal request rates incrementally. Perform validation testing, simulate valid user sessions, transactions, and API calls to validate stability. Check log integrity and configurations to ensure no tampering during mitigation. When stability is established, return monitoring thresholds to pre-attack baselines and reinstitute proactive monitoring.

- Business and Communication Recovery:

Recovery is more than infrastructure; it's trust. Inform customers, partners, and stakeholders of restored services with openness and confidence. Internally evaluate reputational fallout, downtime expense, and customer mood to optimize future response plans.

Example Recovery Timeline:

- Hour 1–3: Containment complete; stabilize core systems.
- Hour 4–8: Phased service restoration, verify user experience.
- Day 1–3: Perform post-recovery audits, report status updates, and return to full operations.

Recovery isn't merely about bringing systems up; it's about restoring confidence, stability, and preparedness for the next storm.

Communication and Stakeholder Management

Information flow, not just network flow, is as important during a DDoS attack. The best technical response can come apart at the seams if communication does not hold up. An orchestrated information approach avoids confusion, upholds confidence, and saves reputation.

- Internal Communication:

Clarity starts inside. Have a clear escalation route from Security Operations to Management to Public Relations (PR). All departments should function together, sharing confirmed updates, not assumptions. Utilize collaboration platforms such as Slack or Microsoft Teams with specific "War Room" channels for real-time coordination. Record all decisions and timestamp critical actions for future reference.

- External Communication

Coordinate with national cyber authorities, CERT, and mitigation vendors to maintain uniform external visibility. In public communication, take the tone of transparency but without alarm. Offer a transparent status to the customer and media with a focus on continuous resolution efforts instead of ambiguity.

Crisis Communication Checklist:

- Have one spokesperson to prevent contradictory statements.
- Prepare pre-approved social media templates for instant communication.
- Keep periodic updates going until complete restoration, even with incremental progress.

Remember: a well-managed story can shield brand trust better than any firewall. Conversely, silence or conflicting messages during an outage can magnify harm beyond the technical impact of the attack.

Forensic Analysis and Post-Incident Review

With systems stabilized, the mission shifts from response to reflection. Each DDoS incident is full of valuable lessons if analyzed with accuracy. Forensic analysis gives raw data a meaningful interpretation, so the same mistake never happens again.

- Forensic Objectives:

Analysts start by defining attack patterns, vectors, and origin networks. Firewall, CDN, WAF, and app server logs are tied together to plot the attack timeline. Packet captures are used to reconstruct the sequence when traffic started spiking, which endpoints were attacked, and how defenses reacted.

- Root Cause Analysis (RCA):

Next, identify the attack type (e.g., SYN flood, DNS amplification, HTTP flood), the exploited infrastructure vulnerabilities, and the effectiveness of mitigation measures. Gauge response times, choke points, and escalation workflow success.

Post-Incident Review Framework:

- What worked: Useful tools, teams, or communication channels.
- What failed: Misconfigurations, slow responses, or vendor shortcomings.
- What to improve: Automation potential, training issues, or monitoring deficiencies.

Hold a cross-team debrief, capturing important lessons in your Incident Response (IR) knowledge base. Refresh playbooks and enforce learning through tabletop exercises.

In cyber defense, each DDoS incident is a practice run for the next, and an unreviewed DDoS incident is a chance lost.

Institutionalizing Learning for Long-Term Resilience

The real trademark of a mature cybersecurity stance is not the speed of reaction, but rather the ability to learn. Resilience is established when ad-hoc responses become repeatable, fact-driven, and institutionalized processes. Each DDoS should hone and not merely test your organization's defense fabric.

Steps for Resilience Maturity

- Embed Learning into DevSecOps Pipelines: Inform every incident's insight into automated defense systems like changing WAF rules, load balancer thresholds, and monitoring triggers without waiting for humans.

- Tabletop Exercises on a Regular Basis: Run a diverse range of DDoS scenarios from high-volume floods to layer-7 stealthy attacks. Benchmark agility, coordination, and communication under simulated pressure.
- Benchmark Response Metrics: Monitor Mean Time to Detect (MTTD) and Mean Time to Recovery (MTTR) to measure improvement over time.
- Develop Institutional Knowledge Bases: Keep playbooks, checklists, FAQs, and case studies in central repositories to inform future responders.
- Connect IR Performance to Business KPIs: Tie technical results to executive metrics uptime, customer trust, and revenue impact.

In the end, resilience isn't so much about preventing DDoS attacks as it is about succeeding in spite of them. Resilient organizations take every attack as a stress test for optimization, with each recovery making the system more robust, quicker, and wiser than the last.

DDoS Response Templates and Checklists

Preparedness loves structure. The following templates serve as response team quick-start guides:

- Quick Response Template:

Detection → Verification → Escalation → Containment → Communication → Recovery.

- Role Assignment Matrix:

Establish definitive ownership within SOC, NOC, DevOps, PR, and Legal for each phase.

- Post-Event Review Template:

Embed metrics, event timeline, RCA summary, and recommendations for improvement.

These templates can be scaled or tailored to startups, enterprises, or ISPs alike to provide clarity amidst chaos and standardization across each battle won in the digital space.

Case Study: "The Midnight Flood"

At 2:13 a.m., an emerging fintech company providing instant microloans detected a sudden spike in traffic. Within minutes, the system dashboard reported a 400 Gbps flood pounding their public APIs. What initially started in confusion in the monitoring room escalated to crisis very soon. The team initially confused the spike as user growth following a viral campaign, losing fifteen critical minutes before they were sure that it was a DDoS attack.

Upon verification, containment measures kicked in. WAF rules and rate limiting slowed incoming connections as the ISP was engaged to allow for upstream filtering. Scrubbing centers were activated, albeit with an initial communications delay to result in partial service loss. The PR department of the company had a difficult time providing timely updates, creating customer confusion on social media.

Nevertheless, earlier tabletop exercises paid dividends. Escalation routes were evident, and automated scripts redirected traffic to backup areas. By morning, services were back online 60% quicker than after a comparable outage months before.

Post-incident, leadership required a complete post-incident review. Playbooks were tightened up, messaging procedures optimized, and real-time alerts synchronized with vendor systems. The incident turned around, shifting the company's defense posture from reaction-induced panic to process-based resiliency.

Beyond Recovery - Toward Preparedness

From preparation to post-incident learning, the DDoS response lifecycle attests to one eternal truth: resilience is constructed, not purchased. Every step of detection, containment, eradication, and recovery depends as much on collaboration and communication as it does on technology.

Chapter 12: Botnet Detection, Tracking, and Takedowns

Introduction: Pursuing the Invisible Enemy

Under the visible net, there exists a darker, more orchestrated realm: the botnet system, the unseen driver behind contemporary Distributed Denial of Service (DDoS) attacks. Botnets, vast networks of hijacked machines, are the substrates of online anarchy, converting ordinary systems to disruption soldiers. From the notorious Mirai botnet that exploited vulnerable IoT cameras to current polymorphic and self-repairing botnets that change so quickly that they outpace defenses, infection scale has turned cyber warfare into an automated struggle. But it's not simply about pulling servers out of power; it's about dismantling infrastructure while discouraging re-emergence. Each successful takedown is a blow against the economy of cybercrime, an indication to attackers that toughness can be achieved. Behind every operation is a meeting of intelligence, law enforcement, ethical considerations, and diplomacy, demonstrating that the battle against botnets is as much human as it is technological.

Botnet Detection Fundamentals

Botnet detection is akin to tracking ripples in a tempest; its constituent packets are no different, but collectively they betray orchestration. Even the first detection systems employed signature-based mechanisms, which recognized malware through familiar code patterns or payload fingerprints. But when botnets adapted, behavioral detection became the norm emphasizing how compromised systems act, not what code they possess. This includes identifying infection patterns, communication frequency, and traffic patterns that fall outside a network's norm.

One key step here is to establish Indicators of Compromise (IoCs). These may be abnormal volumes of outbound traffic, repeated DNS queries, regular beaconing intervals, or packet payloads that are the same on many devices. Analysts use them to correlate infections and determine command-and-control (C2) infrastructures.

This intelligence is supported by honeypots and telemetry sensors, intentionally vulnerable networks that draw botnet traffic and log behavioral data. With deception environments, researchers are able to see infection spreading, payload formatting, and control commands in real time.

Lastly, threat intelligence sharing serves as the world nervous system of detection. Tools such as MISP (Malware Information Sharing Platform) and coordination between CERTs (Computer Emergency Response Teams) facilitate immediate dissemination of IoCs so that what one learns, the world can defend against. In this world of shared observance, detection isn't a solo endeavor; it's a coordinated, worldwide act of cyber self-preservation.

Botnet Fingerprinting: Unmasking the Beast

Most botnets leave a faint, but distinctive digital fingerprint that can be identified, indexed, and employed to track back its ancestry. This fingerprint tends to be in the tiny technical specifics: C2 communication headers, payload format, encryption algorithms, or protocol anomalies. Through their decryption, defenders can recognize a botnet family even when its source code has been altered or re-branded.

Reverse engineering comes into play here. Both static analysis (analysis of binaries without execution) and dynamic analysis (execution of malware under a controlled environment) are carried out by analysts to learn about command syntax, encryption keys, and propagation mechanisms. By these techniques, researchers can identify whether a botnet steals credentials, performs DDoS attacks, mines cryptocurrency, or serves as a proxy network.

Sandboxing and detonation frameworks enable experimentation with safety, seeing how a bot infects, propagates, and communicates with C2 servers without putting real-world spread at risk. Environments such as Cuckoo Sandbox or any other mimic real-world systems to identify behavioral logs, registry changes, and outgoing connections in real time.

Interestingly, code reuse within botnet families aids in the identification of botnet genealogy. Several contemporary variants, ranging from Mirai to Mozi and QakBot, take modules from previous codebases, enabling analysts to track evolutionary trends in much the same way that geneticists analyze DNA mutations.

Cataloging and correlation are not the only goals; discovery is included as well. By means of Information Sharing and Analysis Centers (ISACs) and private cyber research facilities, researchers hold worldwide fingerprint databases, such that when one node of the web sees a pattern it knows, the entire global defense community can react quickly, coordinated, and informed.

Mapping Command-and-Control (C2) Infrastructure

Behind each botnet horde is an unseen structure: the Command-and-Control (C2) infrastructure, the central nervous system that sends commands, collects information, and organizes attacks. Mapping this command center is usually the most important and daunting task in a takedown campaign.

There are a number of C2 models. The centralized model is dependent on a small number of master servers, easy to manage but also to take apart. The peer-to-peer (P2P) model distributes command ability between infected devices; however, this makes disruption much more difficult. Fast-flux architectures utilize dynamically changing DNS records to hide actual server positions, while Domain Generation Algorithms (DGAs) produce thousands of possible C2 domain names per day to avoid blacklists.

To reveal these, threat researchers employ DNS sinkholing, an attack method that diverts malicious domain requests to controlled servers rather than live C2 nodes. Not only does this stop the dissemination of commands, but it also enables researchers to analyze the botnet's extent, infection density, and geographic distribution.

Graph analysis of communications also maps out the structure of C2 networks detecting central hubs, transmission frequencies, and clusters of connections. Rapid-flux detection, where DNS record rotation and TTL anomalies are monitored, uncovers concealed infrastructures masquerading as legitimate services.

The operation frequently reaches the dark web, where botnet administrators are managing operations through hidden TOR-based services, encrypted chat, or bulletproof hosting providers. Through tracking overlapping wallets, reused credentials, and time-zone activity, threat researchers can identify C2 operations with threat actor TTPs (Tactics, Techniques, and Procedures) and attribute activity to known cybercrime actors or state-sponsored units.

A classic case was the Avalanche botnet takedown, a multijurisdictional effort by the FBI, Europol, and more than 40 agencies. Experts charted over 800,000 domains and 500 servers utilized for financial malware and spam operations. The coordinated takedown tore down one of the most enduring botnet infrastructures in the past, providing a model for international, intelligence-driven cyber enforcement.

Mapping C2s is not just technical, it's forensic architecture on a planetary level, where every packet, IP address, and domain uncovers another component of the enemy's anatomy.

Legal Collaboration and Global Enforcement

Disassembling a botnet is not only a technical achievement but a legal and diplomatic endeavor that transcends jurisdictions, laws, and time zones. Botnets, by their nature, are transnational creatures infected hosts could be in one location, command servers in another, and administrators in a third. This fragmentation of jurisdictions frequently discourages concerted takedowns, which demand profound legal synchronization and international confidence.

High-profile successes are an indicator of this synergy. Operation Tovar, the disruption of the GameOver Zeus botnet in 2014, disrupted a giant financial theft scheme through cooperation among the FBI, Europol, and private cybersecurity companies. The Avalanche Network operation in 2016 destroyed a worldwide infrastructure used for phishing and malware propagation that engaged more than 40 nations. Later, the 2021 Emotet takedown, conducted by Europol and coordinated with several law enforcement groups, was a milestone in coordinated cyber enforcement, taking command of hundreds of servers and routing infected machines towards cleanup.

Botmasters employ proxies, encryption, and stacked anonymity networks to hide behind. Where takedowns converge with nation-state activity, diplomacy is as important as code, reducing enforcement from a lawful issue to a geopolitical balancing act in the cyber field of battle.

Sinkholing and Kill Switch Deployment

One of the most effective weapons in a defender's toolkit is sinkholing, a method that diverts botnet traffic from command servers operated by malicious attackers to controlled environments run by researchers. Experts use this method to watch, contain, and occasionally disable active infections without endangering end users.

By examining diverted traffic, teams can approximate the size of a botnet, infection geographics, and behavior in real time.

Technically, sinkholing usually entails DNS redirection, altering domain name records locally to direct to secure IPs or even legitimate BGP hijacks, in which network paths are briefly redirected to keep C2 traffic isolated. These procedures need close coordination between ISPs, domain registrars, and law enforcement since improper management may impact legitimate networks. Controlled response handling guarantees that no sensitive user information is mismanaged under surveillance.

Kill switches are another, frequently more flamboyant, countermeasure, network checks, or lines of code that, when activated, can turn off malware everywhere. Occasionally, these are deliberate backdoors added for developers; sometimes they are inadvertently found.

Yet these interventions are ethically and operationally risky. All sinkholing operations are therefore rigorously tested and legally sanctioned.

After-sinkhole surveillance is still necessary to ensure re-infection vectors are shut down, compromised systems patched, and the botnet cannot evolve into its next form, a standing race between disappearance and mutation in cyberspace.

Ethical and Legal Limitations in Countermeasures

In the murk of cyber war, the distinction between moral defense and virtual vigilantism is all too often dangerously thin. While defenders are forced to act quickly to safeguard networks, they must find their way through the gray of active defense where countervailing measures may cross the line from defense into reprisal. The stabilizing legal principles of necessity, proportionality, and consent undergird legitimate interventions: acts must be necessary to avoid harm, proportionate to the danger, and authorized by authority or ownership.

The contentious concept of counter-hacking, or "hack back," remains contentious among policymakers and practitioners. While it could threaten to bring down malicious infrastructure in short order, its international legal status is unclear. Hitting back across borders could unintentionally damage innocent systems or transgress sovereignty, provoking diplomatic repercussions.

Equally nuanced are implications of data privacy. Defenders who collect or log traffic from compromised hosts compromise civilian rights and privacy safeguards like GDPR. This renders correct disclosure essential; security researchers are urged to coordinate disclosures with vendors, regulators, and CERTs ahead of public release to prevent exploitation but allow remediation.

The international debate on legalizing active defense rages on, with advocates arguing for deterrence and adversary disruption and critics sounding the alarm for escalation and unintended escalations. Without global norms, ethical cyber defense is constrained by restraint, transparency, and cooperation. True art is eliminating digital threats without becoming what one opposes a test of ability but of moral control in an increasingly militarized cyberspace.

Coordinated Takedowns: Anatomy of an Operation

Each successful botnet takedown is a surgical strike, orchestrated on multiple levels of intelligence, technology, and law enforcement. These operations have multiple phases, each needing careful planning and international coordination.

- Phase 1 – Intelligence Gathering: Analysts begin by mapping the topology of the botnet locating C2 servers, clusters of infection, and operational patterns. This includes deep packet inspection, reverse engineering, and penetration of dark web communication channels.
- Phase 2 – Stakeholder Alignment: Coordination across ISPs, hosting services, LEAs, and CERTs guarantees collective effort. Information-sharing procedures and jurisdictional clearances are obtained in this phase.
- Phase 3 – Technical Execution: With warrants and alliances in hand, groups execute domain seizes, sinkholing, or server take-downs. The mission is to disrupt C2 communication without collateral damage.

Phase 4 – Legal Enforcement: Concurrently with technical containment, LEAs make arrests, take digital evidence, and initiate forensic preservation for prosecution. This connects cyber defense to criminal justice.

- Phase 5 – Post-Operation Recovery: Efforts are redirected towards restoring normal services, releasing patch advisories, and coordinating with the media to alert without alarming.

The real success metric, though, isn't merely takedown but resilience when the system itself becomes harder to crack, so the very same threat can't resurface again.

The Future of Botnet Takedowns

The future of botnet takedowns is to move away from reactive containment to proactive disruption. Breakthroughs in AI-powered intelligence automation now make it possible to map and anticipate malicious infrastructures ahead of activation, enabling response preemption. However, the battleground changes, decentralized botnets adopting blockchain-based command infrastructure are on the rise, immune to the old sinkholing or seizure. To defeat these, countries are creating real-time, cross-border cooperation frameworks that integrate data, jurisdiction, and quick action. The next decade will require not only smarter tools but ethical AI and harmonized cyber laws, making defense both effective and fair in an ever-more borderless digital world.

From disorder to precision, every takedown is a triumph of order over chaos. These actions demonstrate that cybersecurity isn't just technology, it's strategy, it's ethics, and it's humanity. Real victory doesn't come through destruction but through taking down digital tyranny, piece by piece, by server, by packet, by operation.

Chapter 13: Cybersecurity Policy Making and Governance Design

Introduction: Governance as the Quiet Guardian

Cybersecurity governance is the organizational scaffolding of digital protection, prescribing how decisions, responsibility, and control structures move throughout an organization. It's not firewalls or packet filters, it's people, processes, and policies working together to make those technologies useful. In DDoS defense specifically, governance makes sure that the response is aligned, practiced, and measurable instead of scattered or improvised.

All organizations spend money on tools, but leave the governance layer that makes those tools align with risk priorities and executive intent in place. Without that layer, even the most sophisticated scrubbing or filtering products falter under ambiguity; nobody knows who sanctions countermeasures, how to alert ISPs, or when to enable failover systems.

This chapter is constructed on three legs of mature governance:

- Frameworks that work with structure and standardization.
- Institutionalization, incorporating resilience into culture.
- KPIs measuring security as performance, rather than perception.

The Foundations of Cybersecurity Governance

In its simplest definition, cybersecurity governance is a control framework that transforms business intent into technically enforceable action. It enableshas leaders hipto establish direction, risk tolerance, and resources, whereas engineers turn these into measurable controls. Effective governance is at the nexus of strategy, compliance, and execution, taking boardroom deliberations and translating them into firewall policies, response playbooks, and audit trails.

Its main elements are:

- Leadership accountability: Unambiguous ownership of cyber risk decisions.
- Policies and standards: Auditable, approved, and written guidelines for security behavior.
- Risk management: Detection, assessment, and mitigation of ever-changing threats such as DDoS.
- Measurement: Establishing metrics that validate protection, detection, and recovery efficiency.

Governance turns "security" from an IT chore that is reactive to an enabler of business. For example, a mid-sized fintech company reduced its Mean Time to Respond (MTTR) by 60% after it established a governance council that inspected incident readiness monthly, matching SOC data with business continuity objectives.

With foundations laid, next comes standardization, embracing models that turn governance into a system that is quantifiable rather than just a philosophy.

Frameworks That Work

Cybersecurity governance should not be based on ad-hoc approaches. To be able to shift defense to discipline, organizations require systematic frameworks that formalize roles, responsibilities, and processes. Such frameworks guarantee repeatability where DDoS readiness is system-oriented rather than personality-dependent. The following global standards and governance models constitute the foundation of institutional cyber resilience.

NIST Cybersecurity Framework

The most commonly cited model for cybersecurity governance is the NIST Cybersecurity Framework (CSF). It structures security functions into five actionable phases: Identify, Protect, Detect, Respond, and Recover.

- Identify: List critical systems and business processes susceptible to loss of availability. In this phase, governance demands an up-to-date asset inventory, a DDoS risk register, and escalation ownership defined.
- Protect: Apply defense mechanisms, rate limiting, firewalls, scrubbing services, and redundant network routes. Policy

checkpoints make sure that safeguards are regularly tested and budgeted.

- Detect: Governance requires active anomaly detection by NetFlow analysis, SOC monitoring, and behavior baselines. Periodic board-level KPI reviews monitor detection latency and false positives.
- Respond: Incident response procedures are tested via tabletop exercises, confirming comms flows, escalation routes, and decision criteria.
- Recover: Governance completes the loop by requiring post-incident reviews and lessons-learned meetings to revise policies and vendor SLAs.

NIST's implementation levels (1–4), Partial to Adaptive, enable organizations to compare their DDoS maturity. Tier 1 companies might have ad hoc measures, whereas Tier 4 organizations automate detection and initiate scrubbing in seconds. The CSF now serves as a governance compass, relating technical capability to executive assurance.

ISO/IEC 27001 + 27035

The ISO/IEC 27001 system specifies the template for an Information Security Management System (ISMS) - a formalized governance framework that makes policies consistent, controlled, and auditable. It is pure governance: a ceaseless plan–implement–monitor–improve loop.

In DDoS protection, ISO 27001 mandates documented controls on risk assessment, access control, vendor management, and service continuity. It sees to it that each configuration or mitigation technique has an owner, a review cycle, and trackable evidence.

Complementing it, ISO/IEC 27035 is more focused on incident management. It prescribes how organizations plan, discover, report, analyze, and react to cyber incidents such as DDoS attacks. For instance, it requires that incident playbooks contain pre-defined thresholds (e.g., 80% bandwidth saturation initiates "Stage 1 response") and that incident records flow into management reviews.

Together, 27001 and 27035 form a feedback-based ecosystem policy that drives control, control drives evidence, and evidence informs ongoing improvement. In a crisis, such governance balance enables Legal, HR, IT, and Communications to move in unison, minimizing downtime and reputation loss.

COBIT 2019 Framework

COBIT 2019 framework fills the gap between IT governance and enterprise value. Governance is defined as the synchronization of business objectives, IT strategies, and stakeholder expectations through five domains: Align, Plan, Build, Run, and Monitor.

In DDoS management, COBIT places uptime, SLA fulfillment, and incident preparedness within the realm of enterprise performance management. It calls for risk appetite, budgeting, and resilience measures to be examined at the board level rather than in IT reports.

For example, within the Monitor domain, COBIT calls for ongoing review of performance metrics such as service availability or attack detection latency. Within the Plan, it calls for risk-driven investments ensuring DDoS mitigation expenditure is proportional to business criticality.

COBIT's strength is translating packet loss percentage to risk exposure terminology that executives comprehend, so that cybersecurity becomes an operating and cost decision rather than a technical one.

CIS Controls

For companies in need of practical, low-complexity governance, the CIS Critical Security Controls (v8) provide a prioritized plan of 18 controls aligned to actual-world threats. Some directly support DDoS readiness:

- Inventory and Asset Control: Retain visibility across all exposed endpoints and IP ranges at risk of exploitation.
- Continuous Vulnerability Management: Identify old firmware or open ports commonly used by botnets.
- Secure Network Settings: Normalize firewall, routing, and access configurations to reduce exposure.

- Incident Response Management: Establish and validate escalation paths for network anomalies and volumetric events.

CIS Controls focus on operational governance; practical measures associated with measurable results. Smaller entities tend to implement CIS to initiate foundational discipline prior to expanding to ISO or NIST models.

NIST SP 800-61 & SP 800-83

Whereas the CSF offers strategic structure, the NIST Special Publications (SP) provide operational depth.

- SP 800-61r2: Computer Security Incident Handling Guide lays out step-by-step procedures for incident response preparation, detection, containment, eradication, recovery, and lessons learned.
- SP 800-83: Guide to Malware Incident Prevention and Handling extends this to botnet management and infection containment.

For DDoS management, these guides are playbook templates. They establish escalation thresholds ("if inbound traffic is 300% above baseline, alert Tier-1 SOC"), containment procedures (null routing, filtering by IP), and emphasize interoperability between SOC and management reporting systems.

When combined with corporate governance layers, SP 800-series standards guarantee that detection notices prompt not only technical actions, but policy-level responsibility such as mandatory CISO reports or automated incident recording for audit preparedness.

They are governance-in-action policies made operational.

CMMC and Sectoral Regulations

In addition to frameworks, compliance-driven governance introduces enforceability.

Cybersecurity Maturity Model Certification (CMMC), specific to U.S. defense contractors, codifies maturity at 5 levels: basic hygiene through advanced, adaptive capabilities. It integrates governance accountability through evidence-based audits.

GDPR (Europe) and NIS2 Directive also mandate demonstrable resilience and reporting incidents, such as DDoS impacts. Such mandates connect technical controls with legal obligations and enforce governance maturity.

Finally, effective governance is twofold: audit preparedness and operational robustness making compliance investments at the same time that they build uptime and trust.

Synthesis: Selecting the Appropriate Blend

There is no one framework for all. Effective cybersecurity governance tends to combine the strategic direction of NIST CSF, the discipline of ISO 27001, and the working flexibility of CIS Controls. The secret is risk-based adoption mapping controls to organizational complexity, threat posture, and regulatory risk.

Governance needs to change dynamically, informed by threat intelligence and post-incident feedback loops. As DDoS and botnet strategies become more adaptive, so must governance evolve from frozen documentation into a living system of measurement, accountability, and ongoing readiness.

Governance as Proactive Defense

Governance acts as the operational backbone that binds policy to execution. It transforms "what to do when attacked" into "how to ensure we're never caught unprepared."

The example layers below show how organizations can make DDoS resilience operational as a matter of structured control, supervision, and ongoing testing.

From Reactive to Proactive Structures

Organizations act primarily in response to a DDoS incident, revealing vulnerabilities, frantically reaching out to ISPs, engaging mitigation appliances, and issuing ad-hoc statements. This reactive process leads to longer outages, muddy lines of authority, and recurring post-incident uncertainty.

Governance alters this dynamic. A mature program installs expectation through established, regular procedures not improvisation. Scheduled stress tests confirm that detection systems and failover designs actually work as planned. Red-team DDoS drills reproduce attack conditions, exercising network resilience, but also decision speed and escalation tempo.

For instance, certain businesses enforce monthly scrubbing tests by policy-orchestrated drills in which scrubbing centers, SOC analysts, and vendors certify mitigation flow end-to-end. Performance from these exercises (packet loss, detection latency, recovery time) is fed into quarterly governance reviews, so defense readiness is never taken for granted; it's always demonstrated.

The Cybersecurity Steering Committee

Institutional management starts with a Cybersecurity Steering Committee, the central governing force for resiliency. Its membership usually consists of the CISO, CIO, SOC Head, Risk Officer, and Communications Lead.

The committee combines technical telemetry with executive management. It doesn't run day-to-day; it provides direction. Its charter involves establishing allowable downtime targets, sanctioning DDoS mitigation expenditures, and examining quarterly technical team KPIs.

Policy Instruments

Good governance relies on written, version-controlled policies that codify response behavior. Key instruments are:

- DDoS Response Policy – Establishes trigger thresholds, response levels, escalation chains, and communication protocols.
- Vendor SLA Governance Policy – Defines uptime commitments, failover dependencies, and performance expectations for third-party mitigation vendors.
- Communication Escalation Matrix – Defines who tells what to whom during an incident, technical updates to SOC, business updates to leadership, and public statements through PR.
- Post-Incident Review Policy – Requires documentation of lessons learned, root cause mapping, and continuous improvement activities.

Every policy has to trace back to some formal framework control, e.g., ISO 27001 A.17.1 (Information Security Continuity), to be auditable. Governance guarantees these documents stay as living documents, reviewed on a yearly basis or after each major incident.

Institutionalized Drills and Tabletop Exercises

Governance converts simulation from a best practice to a compliance requirement. Quarterly DDoS tabletop exercises are performed by organizations with SOC engineers, IT ops, communications, and executive teams. The drills metric critical KPIs like time to detection, time to mitigation, and decision latency.

After-action reports are recorded, cleared by the steering committee, and followed to closure through documented improvement plans. The end result is a closed governance loop, preparation, validation, correction, and revalidation that injects readiness into culture, and not just documentation.

With time, this cycle makes DDoS defense reflexive, predictable, and ever-changing.

KPIs for Cybersecurity Aligning Technical and Executive Oversight

Quantification lends credibility to cybersecurity. Engineers talk in packets and logs, but executives hear numbers, ratios, and performance curves. What fills this communication gap is well-defined Key Performance Indicators (KPIs) translating technical activity into quantifiable business results. They turn DDoS defense into a strategic performance function that can be viewed, optimized, and justified, rather than a reactive cost center.

Designing Metrics That Matter

Successful cybersecurity measurement starts by dividing Operational Metrics from Governance KPIs.

Operational Metrics capture the effectiveness of technical defense:

- Average Detection Latency: The speed at which anomalous traffic is detected.
- Mitigation Efficiency: Proportion of malicious packets blocked without impacting legitimate users.
- Mean Time to Respond (MTTR): Time taken between detection and normal service restoration.

Collectively, these KPIs integrate operational excellence with leadership visibility, translating incident reports into strategic insight.

Linking KPIs to Executive Dashboards

Contemporary government relies on data visualization and automation. Data from SIEMs, NOCs, WAFs, and traffic analyzers should automatically be fed into executive dashboards constructed with such tools as Power BI, Grafana, or Splunk.

These dashboards need to bridge cyber KPIs with business indicators for instance, correlating DDoS downtime with SLA penalties or churn rates of customers.

By having the CISO provide current data in conjunction with financial metrics, security becomes a measurable aspect of business performance, its executive scrutiny and investment guaranteed.

Governance Audit and Feedback Loop

Each KPI informs a cycle of continuous improvement. Post-incident analytics and quarterly reviews must deepen response thresholds, revise playbooks, and detect skill gaps. Governance requires each incident no matter how small to make the next response better. Metrics become lessons, and lessons become resilience.

Combining Governance with Technical Operations

Governance works only when it's integrated into the day-to-day operating DNA of the organization. Policy and frameworks must be reflected in the tools, automation scripts, and daily routine of security teams.

Integration begins in the DevSecOps pipeline, where governance rules enforce security scanning, patch validation, and configuration baselines prior to deployment. Network monitoring systems and SIEMs should react with the governance triggers and, for example, automatically escalate anomalies that go above defined thresholds to the CISO dashboard or incident management system.

Governance also holds vendors accountable via SLA dashboards, with measurable uptime delivered by mitigation partners. Redundancy practices and failover verification should be formalized into regular health tests, not the occasional review.

It prevents governance from being merely within documentation; it resides within every packet, every dashboard, and every automated defensive action.

Case Example: Governance in Action

One regional bank experienced three large-scale DDoS attacks over six months, resulting in multi-hour disruptions and customer complaints. After the crisis, the bank established a Cyber Risk Governance Board headed by its Chief Information Security Officer and Chief Risk Officer.

They implemented the NIST Cybersecurity Framework to standardize response phases, instituted quarterly DDoS training drills, and mandated monthly KPI reviews in all branches. Vendor agreements were rewritten with SLA penalties based on mitigation time and uptime.

In one year, the bank decreased unplanned downtime by 70%, enhanced detection accuracy, and set transparent reporting to regulators.

The change was cultural management came from paperwork to an operating rhythm. Every group, from SOC analysts to executives, knew that resilience was no longer a response; it was a responsibility.

Challenges in Governance Implementation

It is much simpler in theory to establish a governance structure than it is in reality. Organizations have cultural and structural resistance to change; teams view governance as bureaucracy that hinders innovation or operational velocity. Overlapping mandates in IT, compliance, and risk departments contribute to confusion regarding ownership and accountability during cyber breaches.

Budgeting becomes another point of friction security investments are unlikely to drive immediate ROI, causing reluctance at the executive level. Additionally, data privacy regulations make ongoing monitoring difficult, as user or employee data gathered for threat detection could create compliance issues.

The solution is in creating a cross-functional governance charter, ratified from the top down. This charter needs to clearly lay out roles, communication channels, and escalation procedures. When governance is framed not as control but as enablement, a means of creating safe, unbroken operations resistance dissipates and alignment increases among departments and layers of leadership.

Future of Cyber Governance

The future of cybersecurity governance will be characterized by automation, flexibility, and consolidation.

AI-based policy enforcement will make compliance scoring automatic, assessing whether configurations, patch levels, and response times are compliant with governance requirements in real time. Dynamic governance models will change controls continuously based on real-time threat intelligence, turning static structures into living systems.

Above all, resilience itself will become a business KPI, monitored in parallel with revenue and uptime. Boards will judge cyber performance, not on the lack of incidents, but on the speed and consistency of recovery. Governance will therefore transition from a compliance requirement to a source of competitive advantage, a signature of mature digital organizations.

Summary: Governance as the Backbone of Cyber Resilience

Organizations that are well-governed are prepared to be attacked, integrate flawlessly in times of crisis, and evolve continuously afterward.

Governance's ultimate aim is predictability in adversity, knowing precisely who acts, when, and how, before the first packet hits the perimeter.

Against DDoS and in general, governance is the quiet architecture of power: not jazzy, not after-the-fact, but intentional, quantifiable, and long-lasting.

Chapter 14: Legal Compliance and Ethical Imperatives

Introduction: The Law at the Edge of Cyberspace

As the virtual front expands, so too does the combat zone of legality. Distributed Denial of Service (DDoS) attacks push against not only technological limits but also the law and moral frameworks that shape cyberspace. Bytes may cross borders freely, but laws are still confined within jurisdictions. The consequence is a complicated, frequently fissured terrain of enforcement where what is a "cyberattack" in one country is a "network test" in another.

This chapter delves into the twin pillars that support contemporary cyber defense: legal compliance and ethical duty.

The Global Legal Landscape of Cybercrime

The battle against DDoS is international, but legislation regarding it is inharmoniously allocated. The Computer Fraud and Abuse Act (CFAA) of the United States continues to be one of the most cited laws, penalizing unauthorized access and service disruption. Within the European Union, the GDPR indirectly affects DDoS response by way of data privacy restrictions, and the NIS2 Directive compels increased resilience as well as reporting of breaches. India's Information Technology Act, Singapore's Cybersecurity Act, and Australia's Critical Infrastructure Security Framework all provide regional shades. For defenders, this involves traversing a mosaic of national legislations while remaining operationally ready globally, a tricky balance between compliance and capability.

ISP Liability and Shared Responsibility

Internet Service Providers (ISPs) are in a legally vulnerable position. On the one hand, they are carriers of connectivity; on the other, they can be unwittingly involved as accomplices in DDoS campaigns when their infrastructure is abused. The issue here is to what extent ISPs should be held responsible for attacks that pass through their networks?

All jurisdictions treat ISPs as "common carriers," with the protection that they cannot be held directly liable if they are acting in good faith and employ reasonable mitigation. This immunity is not, however, absolute. The regulators in the EU and the UK have promoted proactive monitoring obligations, while the U.S. takes a light hand, focusing on privacy and neutrality.

ModernContemporary legal thinking leans towards collaborative responsibility: ISPs should apply simple mitigation (e.g., rate limits, ingress filtering, abuse response teams) but not monitor each packet. Ethical responsibility is to protect without crossing the line, preventing the defense of one user from becoming the surveillance of another.

Attribution and Prosecution Challenges

It is notoriously hard to attribute a DDoS attack to a particular actor. Attackers usually direct their traffic via botnets, VPNs, proxy chains, or hijacked infrastructure across several jurisdictions. This technical complexity poses a major legal challenge to prosecution.

Courts need evidence to a criminal standard beyond a reasonable doubt, and yet the digital trail of a DDoS will infrequently qualify. Attackers could employ reflective amplification, where it looks like the attack was started by innocent systems.

In order to counter these gaps, emerging global initiatives such as the UN Open-Ended Working Group on Cybersecurity attempt to normalize norms and foster real-time collaboration. Still, for defenders, the naked reality is that prevention consistently runs ahead of punishment.

Privacy vs. Security: The Ethical Dilemma

In their effort to protect networks, organizations tend to gather huge amounts of information traffic logs, user metadata, and behavioral fingerprints. But surveillance for security can quite easily pass into surveillance of privacy. The distinction between monitoring for protection and profiling for control is perilously thin.

Look at theto the use of deep packet inspection (DPI) to identify malicious payloads. While effective against DDoS patterns, DPI could disclose private content, putting it at odds with privacy legislation such as the GDPR and the CCPA.

The overarching principle has to be proportionality; security measures have to be no more invasive than is required to reach defense goals. Transparency in data processing, log anonymization, and frameworks of user consent assist in preserving public confidence.

As cybersecurity becomes a civic infrastructure, defenders have inherited moral responsibilities once the province of governments: to safeguard the citizenry without infringing on their rights. The ethical defender doesn't act as a digital vigilante but as a protector of faith, making sure that security is never used as a basis for spying.

Responsible Disclosure and the Ethics of Hacking

The hacking ethics have changed profoundly from the iconoclastic search of the early days of cyber culture tonow the formalized models of responsible disclosure and bug bounty schemes. Ethical hackers are today a legitimate force within the defense systems of corporate entities, assisting organizations in identifying vulnerabilities before enemies can do so.

Yet even the distinction between "ethical" and "illegal" remains one of context. In the CFAA, even testing a public API without authorization is arguable as illegal access. Acknowledging this, most countries are implementing "safe harbor" provisions for well-intentioned researchers.

Researchers should not harm or expose users in their testing, and companies are expected to act decisively and without reprisal.

The rise of coordinated vulnerability disclosure platforms (Bugcrowd, HackerOne) is an evolved ethical model channeling curiosity into positive security. It embeds a cultural shift: defense is no longer secrete-keeping, but mutually assured resilience.

Offensive Defense and Legal Grey Zones

The idea, popularly referred to as "hack back," contains the ever-present tension between justified self-defense and unjustified revenge. It poses a challenging question: when a botnet overwhelms your network and takes down your services, do you have the right or even the duty to retaliate?

Legally, the answer remains largely unequivocal. In most jurisdictions, active retaliation violates computer misuse, unauthorized access, and digital property protection laws. Statutes such as the Computer Fraud and Abuse Act (CFAA) in the United States, the UK Computer Misuse Act (1990), and equivalent frameworks worldwide explicitly prohibit accessing or altering systems without consent, even when such actions are undertaken with defensive intent. The reason is straightforward but profound: letting people or companies undertake counterstrikes threatens to create cyberspace into a lawless battleground lacking either watchfulness or responsibility.

Ethically, nonetheless, there is no consensus yet. Proponents of offensive defense claim that passive measures alone do not suffice against persistent, state-sponsored, or economically motivated attackers. They advocate methods such as beaconing documents (injecting traceable markers), digital watermarking, or controlled counter-hacks as proportionate and strategic reactions that act as deterrents. To them, restraint against repeated aggression may deter lesser attackers but encourage greater ones and continue impunity.

Critics respond that even the best intentions of such actions threaten collateral harm, infecting innocent intermediary infrastructure, undermining legitimate infrastructure, or inciting diplomatic strife. Critics state that ethical defense is not determined by capability but by constraint: adherence to legality even in the face of provocation. Due process and international law take precedence over the desire for digital retribution.

International Cooperation and Legal Harmonization

Global cooperation remains the most important component of successful cyber defense. Europol's Joint Cybercrime Action Taskforce (J-CAT) and the Cyber Threat Alliance (CTA) are the pinnacles of cooperation through cooperative intelligence. Harmonization, however, is foiled by geopolitics, sovereignty considerations, and uneven legal standards.

Countries vary not only in their definitions of cybercrime, but also in the priority they assign to it. DDoS is considered a criminal annoyance by some states; others consider it a national security threat. Unclear definitions make extradition, sharing of evidence, and coordinated takedowns more difficult.

To multinational companies and ISPs, this translates into creating matrices of compliance charting each operational jurisdiction against local cyber legislation, privacy rules, and reporting obligations for incidents. Global defense ironically starts with local awareness of the law.

The Ethics of Automation and AI in Cyber Defense

Automation has rewritten the pace of cyber response. Machine learning algorithms can now identify anomalies and trigger mitigation in under milliseconds, frequently quicker than human monitoring can respond. But this velocity brings moral perils.

When algorithms choose to halt traffic, quarantine hosts, or quarantine IP blocks, they exercise unconscious power. False positives have the potential to isolate entire communities, and biased data sets can misclassify innocent actors as threats. The emergence of autonomous defense poses a threat to the principle of human responsibility.

Ethical use of AI in cybersecurity requires explainability, auditability, and human-in-the-loop governance. Decision models must be clear and reversible. Companies need to document not just what their systems protect against but why.

The intersection of law and machine learning will shortly set the stage for a new age of algorithmic compliance where regulatory regimes measure not just the result but the reasoning behind defense. In that vision, ethical coding is as critical as ethical behavior.

Case Study: The Mirai Botnet and Cross-Border Prosecution

In 2016, the Mirai botnet launched one of the most disruptive waves of DDoS attacks in history against DNS provider Dyn and left access to Twitter, Netflix, and Reddit paralyzed. The subsequent investigation revealed the complex knot of international jurisdiction and online anonymity.

The culprits, U.S.-based college students, had infected millions of IoT devices around the world. Their malware exploited default weak passwords, turning harmless cameras and routers into cyber weapons. Tracing it back, the prosecution not only relied on technical forensics but on inter-agency collaboration across three continents.

Mirai's aftermath shaped new legal doctrines: device manufacturers were held accountable for shipping insecure products, and nations began drafting IoT security certification laws. The case remains a watershed moment illustrating how liability, ethics, and innovation intersect in cyber defense.

It proved a critical truth: cyber resilience is not just an engineering goal but a legal and moral one.

Toward a Code of Cyber Ethics

The cyber world has no Geneva Convention. There are no internationally ratified rules of engagement, no treaties on the proportional use of cyber force. But as cyber defense evolves, there is an urgent need for ethical codification.

Upcoming proposals suggest a "Cyber Defense Charter," an optional regime establishing rules of responsible behavior:

- Respect for privacy and human rights.
- Prohibition of indiscriminate or retaliatory attacks.
- Transparency of defensive automation.
- Commitment to worldwide cooperation and responsible disclosure.

Institutions such as the Global Forum on Cyber Expertise (GFCE) and CyberPeace Institute are leading such a debate. Ethical maturity, they contend, is the real indicator of cyber power.

The Moral Firewall

Technology protects systems; ethics protects civilization.

In a world where algorithms patrol borders and automation influences judgment, the real firewall is human conscience. The DDoS defender of the future must not only be able to dominate packets and protocols, but principles and purpose.

Chapter 15: The Shifting Threatscape

Introduction: The Next Horizon

With the dust finally settled on decades of cyber skirmishes, the DDoS battlefield is again shifting. The advent of AI-driven autonomy, 5G saturation, edge computing, and quantum cryptography ushers in a new dynamic. The attacker is no longer an anonymous amateur but an automated ecosystem with adaptation and self-learning potential. The defender, meanwhile, is equipping himself with predictive insight and decentralized design.

This chapter surveys the future of DDoS threats and mitigation from AI-driven botnets to defense automation and looks ahead to how the arms race in cyberspace will develop over the next ten years. It is not so much a prediction as a call to readiness: to expect, to plan, and to guide the evolution of defense ahead of the next wave of disruption.

AI-Powered Botnets: The Emergence of Synthetic Intelligence

Classic botnets were crude tools, massive fleets of hijacked machines performing preprogrammed instructions. The next-gen botnets, though, will be sophisticated, autonomous, and AI-based. With the incorporation of machine learning, attackers can create botnets that scan network activity in real time, adapt attack vectors dynamically, and pattern their traffic to appear legitimate to avoid detection.

Examples are:

- Reinforcement learning evasion bots learn to adapt based on firewall feedback and change attack timing or payload.
- Generative adversarial networks (GANs) mimicking authentic web requests to flood WAFs.
- Swarm intelligence enables distributed decision-making for bots and does away with centralized C2 servers.

This shift renders signature-based detection outdated. The distinction between authentic user activity and synthetic attack behavior will become overwhelmingly blurred.

The defenders will thus have to adopt AI vs. AI warfare and deploy their own smart models for predictive analytics, behavioral baselining, and anomaly detection. The ethical ramifications will run deeper as autonomous defensive systems start making split-second choices that affect global connectivity and privacy.

5G and IoT: Scale Beyond Comprehension

The rollout of 5G networks will link billions of devices, most of which are inherently insecure. Each smart bulb, sensor, and car becomes a possible node in the next generation of botnets.

In contrast to legacy internet infrastructure, 5G decentralizes compute, shifting processing to the edge. While enhancing latency, this disperses visibility and makes centralized protection harder. A hijacked IoT cluster on a smart city's edge network might initiate a hyper-localized DDoS that brings down critical services such as traffic management or healthcare IoT infrastructure.

In addition, 5G's bandwidth and speed allow unprecedented volumetric attacks in terms of terabits per second, rather than gigabits.

The problem is in juggling the efficiency of edge computing with the need for distributed, lightweight defensive measures. Next-generation ISPs and regulators will need to implement security-by-design frameworks for IoT vendors and require firmware integrity, remote patching, and anomaly monitoring as defaults.

Edge Computing and Decentralized Battlefields

The progression towards edge computing has reconfigured the very geography of cyberspace. In the past, computation and protection were huge centralized data centers, and core networks were both the functional center and the protection wall of digital ecosystems. But with latency requirements, user demands, and IoT ubiquity pushing processing near the source of data, that structure is eroding. The new battlefront is not a clearly defined periphery; it is a distributed network of micro-environments, each executing, processing, and relaying key operations in real-time.

In such an environment, attack and defense dynamics are splintered. Each factory sensor, retail kiosk, autonomous vehicle, and smart camera on the edge is both an operational gain and a likely avenue of attack. The sheer number and variety of these nodes render traditional centralized monitoring ineffective. Attackers can leverage local vulnerabilities, unpatched firmware, default credentials, or insecure APIs to establish footholds in micro-environments, frequently before central security systems can identify any anomalies.

Edge nodes themselves can also be turned into weapons or shields. Compromised, they can be DDoS attack amplifiers, leveraging their low-latency network proximity to flood adjacent infrastructure. In contrast, when securely accessed, edge nodes can serve as defense isolation points soaking up, filtering, and even misleading attacks before the threat is presented to core systems. This dual nature renders edge computing both a risk multiplier and a resilience opportunity.

To evolve, the defense strategy needs to become decentralized intelligence. Instead of depending on centralized analytics pipelines, organizations are adopting federated AI models in distributed systems in which every edge node learns locally from its context and feeds insights into a global defense model without exchanging raw data. This method maintains privacy, reduces latency, and enables defense mechanisms to be scaled across millions of nodes.

This "distributed vigilance" is an analogy for biological systems: just as the human immune system sends defense cells throughout the body, a decentralized cyber-immune network sends intelligent agents throughout the infrastructure. Each agent identifies anomalies, exchanges indicators of compromise (IoCs), and together tightens the system's resilience.

Edge security, however, cannot be based on algorithms alone. It will be built on top of hardware trust, secure booting mechanisms, zero-trust networking, and ongoing authentication. The edge DDoS defense of the future will depend on partnerships among hardware vendors, service providers, and AI researchers to develop systems that can defend themselves without human intervention, recover gracefully, and learn continuously.

Quantum Computing: Shattering the Locks of Today

Quantum computing will undermine the very cryptographic underpinnings that protect today's communication channels. When quantum supremacy reaches maturity, encryption protocols such as RSA and ECC can be hacked to uncover DDoS mitigation controls, authentication infrastructure, and even TLS-protected traffic inspection layers.

Quantum-armed attackers might be able to decrypt traffic streams in real-time, evading regular rate-limiting or signature-based defenses.

To offset this, post-quantum cryptography (PQC) studies have become a worldwide priority. Defenders must transition to quantum-resistant protocols, re-encrypt network management planes, and authenticate hardware trust anchors.

The shift will not be sudden. For decades, hybrid models merging traditional and quantum-resistant algorithms will coexist. In this period, quantum-enhanced assaults will push the boundaries of encryption and detection, requiring a new generation of cryptographic agility.

Nation-State and Hybrid Warfare

DDoS attacks are no longer weapons of protest or gain; they are instruments of geopolitical maneuver. Nation-states now launch DDoS campaigns to disable communications, financial networks, and critical infrastructure in times of conflict.

These are frequently hybrid attacks, combining cyber and physical disruption like hitting emergency networks during a political crisis or camouflaging espionage operations with mass outages.

Attribution is still a nightmare; attackers make use of worldwide proxy infrastructures and hired-out botnets to hide origin.

Future defense measures will thus have to incorporate cyber diplomacy, attribution models, and international agreements that put mass-scale DDoS attacks in the category of acts of aggression. Cyber defense blocs similar to digital NATO agreements will become pivotal to sustaining worldwide digital stability.

DDoS-as-a-Service: The Commercialization of Chaos

The underground economy has commoditized DDoS as never before. With a few dollars, anyone can hire botnets, select victims, and deploy huge attacks complete with customer support and success metrics.

With increasing automation and cloud anonymity, DDoS-as-a-Service (DaaS) will expand into plug-and-play platforms driven by smart contracts and privacy coins. Payment verification and delivery will be decentralized, allowing attribution to become virtually impossible.

This disruption commercialization follows legitimate SaaS models, scaling and sustaining cybercrime.

It can only be stopped by global financial surveillance collaboration, marketplaces' takedowns, and pervasive affiliate monetization model attacks. Essentially, defenders need to disrupt the economics of DDoS, not packets alone.

AI-Driven Defense Automation

The defense community is not resting. AI is revolutionizing how defenders anticipate, identify, and react to attacks.

Current mitigation systems are transforming from fixed filters to autonomous response engines that process telemetry in real time and deploy countermeasures automatically.

Examples:

- Predictive mitigation: AI algorithms predict attack probability based on past telemetry.
- Autonomous routing: Infrastructure reroutes traffic to scrubbing centers dynamically.
- Self-healing architectures: Networks reconfigure routes or expand cloud nodes to absorb impact.

But such automation poses ethical and operational threats. Over-zealous reactions may exclude legitimate users, interfere with services, or inflict self-categorized outages.

Thus, the second generation of defense needs to marry human-in-the-loop insight, combining automation with human guidance, assuring equilibrium between velocity and accuracy.

Ethical and Legal Frontiers

As both cyber offense and defense grow dominated by AI and automation, the boundaries of responsibility and intent get confused in unprecedented ways. In a classic cyberattack, attribution, although challenging, was at least based on human decision-making. Someone or a group of people had started the act, and liability could theoretically be traced. But what if an autonomous defense system chooses to quarantine an essential medical network because it misidentifies emergency communication as malicious traffic? What if the self-learning botnet, programmed exclusively for penetration testing, gets beyond the control of its creator and starts attacking the actual targets?

These are not abstract questions; they are a necessary outcome of the AI arms race playing out in cybersecurity. As systems self-optimizing and self-guiding become more prevalent, human purpose gets blurred across layers of automation, data, and learning algorithms. The outcome is a legal gray area where present frameworks based on human agency do not go far enough.

What the world now needs is a legal and ethical framework for "cyber autonomy." This entails:

- Digital intent decides if an autonomous system's action is malicious, negligent, or accidental.
- Machine accountability, attributing blame when AI inflicts harm without explicit human control.
- Algorithmic transparency, making sure AI models employed in cybersecurity are auditable, explainable, and governable.

Governments, researchers, and business corporations need to come together to create standards of ethical use of AI in digital defense. These standards will need to ensure that automated systems are auditable, bias-free, and fail-safe in design. Ethical review boards like those for regulating biotechnology or aviation can become the norm soon to clear AI-based defensive systems before deployment at scale.

The moral dilemma is not just a question for law but for philosophy: if AI systems can protect networks more quickly and better than people, is it moral not to utilize them, even with inherent risks? And yet, if these systems can be autonomous and unpredictable, are we merely taking one kind of chaos and substituting another?

Lacking strong governance, tomorrow's defensive AI may end up as combustible and opaque as the criminal systems it is meant to counter. The cybersecurity community must thus adopt responsible innovation, infusing ethics into code, transparency into design, and humanity into automation. The future of digital warfare will not merely challenge our technology; it will challenge our moral compass.

The Cyber Arms Race: Infinity in Motion

The cyber world is trapped in a cycle of continuous escalation. Each innovation in defense either AI-based detection, quantum-resistant encryption, or decentralized design necessarily leads to an innovation in attack approach. The cycle is self-sustaining, akin to the dynamics of nuclear deterrence during the 20th century: innovation spawns counter-innovation.

Today's arms race happens at machine pace. Attackers employ generative AI to design polymorphic malware that evolves with each use. Defenders counter with adaptive machine learning algorithms that can identify unknown patterns. New counter-countermeasures emerge within hours. The outcome is a digital infinity loop a war of algorithms with no end, only continuous adaptation.

But this constant competition also gives birth to opportunity. Defenders can tap into greater telemetry, worldwide collaboration, and autonomous intellect than ever before. Federated learning, open-source intelligence exchange, and cloud-scale analytics power near-real-time global coordination of response. Reactive defense is being converted to predictive resilience, the capacity to predict and negate risks before they materialize.

But the challenge is not technology, but resilience. Organizations holding fixed, compliance-driven security positions will be outperformed by threats that can innovate freely and quickly. The real power of a defender in today's world does not rest in the thickness of their firewall but in their rate of change.

To thrive in this limitless cycle, cybersecurity will need to embrace the practices of biological adaptation, ongoing learning, distributed intelligence, and cooperative survival. Societies, not corporations in isolation, will shape the future of resilience. Threat information will be traded between nations, private companies, and open networks, coalescing into a collective defensive fabric greater than any one entity.

Finally, the cyber arms race is a contest no human can "win." It is an infinite balancing act, a balancing act of innovation versus exploitation. But to win, in the best sense of the term, is to keep balance moving forward just quickly enough to remain ahead, giving away knowledge rather than keeping it for oneself, and exercising power responsibly.

In this infinity of movement, adaptation is immortality. Those that are able to evolve and not simply respond will determine the line between chaos and command.

Conclusion: Weathering the Unseen Future

This tempest that lies ahead will not be battled with firewalls and filters but with vision, ethics, and cooperation.

As the attackers become autonomous entities, so should our defenses become adaptive, intelligent, and ethical systems.

Each DDoS packet, each botnet, and each disruption is a mirror reflecting our collective preparedness.

The future belongs to those who can see the unseen and act before the first wave crashes.

Resilience is not mere survival, it is evolution. The defenders who grasp this reality will not simply survive the future; they will create it.

Appendices

1. https://www.radware.com/cyberpedia/ddospedia/ddos-meaning-what-is-ddos-attack/

2. https://www.netscout.com/blog/why-do-hackers-use-ddos-attacks#:~:text=Distributed%20denial%2Dof%2Dservice%20(,financial%20motivator%20is%20competitive%20takeout.

3. https://en.wikipedia.org/wiki/DDoS_attacks_on_Dyn#:~:text=On%20October%2021%2C%202016%2C%20three%20consecutive%20distributed,of%20users%20in%20Europe%20and%20North%20America.

4. https://www.a10networks.com/blog/5-most-famous-ddos-attacks/#:~:text=On%20Feb.%2028%2C%202018%2C%20GitHub%2C%20a%20platform,across%20tens%20of%20thousands%20of%20unique%20endpoints.%E2%80%9D

5. https://www.paloaltonetworks.com/cyberpedia/what-is-botnet#:~:text=A%20botnet%20(short%20for%20%E2%80%9Crobot,data%20theft%2C%20and%20spam%20distribution.

6. https://solidwp.com/blog/botnets-what-are-they-and-how-do-they-operate/#:~:text=Client%2Dserver%20and%20Peer%2Dto%2Dpeer:%20The%20Architecture%20of%20a,also%20most%20web%20applications%20take%20advantage%20of.

7. https://www.radware.com/cyberpedia/bot-management/botnet/

8. https://www.varonis.com/blog/what-is-c2

9. https://www.netscout.com/blog/top-9-challenges-associated-ddos-mitigation-efforts

10. https://www.broadbandsearch.net/blog/isp-data-privacy-compliance#:~:text=Data%20Subject%20Rights:%20The%20GDPR,to%20opt%20in%20or%20out.

11. https://www.a10networks.com/blog/what-service-providers-and-enterprises-need-to-know-about-ddos-scrubbing-services/#:~:text=A%20portal%20for%20tenants%20where%20each%20tenant,DDoS%20scrubbing%20service%20before%20reaching%20the%20servers.

12. https://jumpcloud.com/it-index/what-is-an-isac-information-sharing-and-analysis-center

13. https://www.radware.com/cyberpedia/application-security/application-layer-ddos layer-7/#:~:text=Conclusion%20Application%20layer%20or%20Layer%207%20DDoS,be%20launched%20against%20a%20website%20or%20application.

14. https://www.f5.com/glossary/owasp

15. https://www.f5.com/labs/articles/threat-intelligence/ddos-against-a-financial-service-analysis-of-a-massive-attack

16. https://platform.sh/company/press/black-friday-is-biggest-week-in-ecommerce/
17. https://www.scayle.com/library/blog/black-friday-ecommerce/
18. https://www.radware.com/blog/application-protection/how-bad-bots-are-disrupting-black-friday-sales/
19. https://arxiv.org/abs/2103.01748
20. https://www.radware.com/cyberpedia/bot-management/bot-protection/
21. https://blog.gigamon.com/2019/09/17/ipfix-vs-netflow/#:~:text=Both%20IPFIX%20and%20NetFlow%20are,to%20billing%20to%20general%20security.
22. https://www.whatsupgold.com/network-traffic-monitoring/sflow#:~:text=sFlow%20is%20a%20multi%2Dvendor%2C%20packet%20sampling%20technology,dedicated%20hardware%20chips%20embedded%20in%20the%20router/switch.
23. https://www.netscout.com/blog/top-9-challenges-associated-ddos-mitigation-efforts
24. https://ddos-guard.net/blog/traffic-filtering-methods
25. https://www.akamai.com/glossary/what-is-blackhole-routing#:~:text=Remote%20triggered%20blackhole%20(RTBH)%20routing,a%20specific%20destination%20IP%20address.

26. https://www.imperva.com/resources/ebooks/Playbook-The-Network-Ops-DDoS-Playbook-new.pdf

27. https://network-insight.net/2015/12/15/bgp-flowspec/

28. https://www.fbi.gov/news/stories/gameover-zeus-botnet-disrupted

29. https://www.mdpi.com/2073-431X/13/1/27#:~:text=6

30. cloudflare.com/learning/ddos/glossary/web-application-firewall-waf/#:~:text=A%20WAF%20or%20web%20application,and%20SQL%20injection%2C%20among%20others.

31. https://spectralops.io/blog/top-10-infrastructure-as-code-iac-tools-to-know-in-2022/#:~:text=3.%20AWS%20CloudFormation%20AWS's%20own%20CloudFormation%20(,and%20covers%20DevOps'%20needs%20and%20best%20practices.

32. https://salt.security/blog/salt-customer-attack-case-study-blocking-a-low-rate-per-bot-http-ddos-attack

33. https://www.mdpi.com/2227-7390/11/1/233#:~:text=Attacks%20such%20as%20DDoS%20are%20a%20threat,with%20malicious%20traffic%2C%20thus%20rendering%20them%20unusable.

34. https://www.paloaltonetworks.in/cyberpedia/what-is-a-threat-intelligence-platform

35. https://www.theguardian.com/technology/2016/oct/26/ddos-attack-dyn-mirai-

botnet#:~:text=Dyn%20estimated%20that%20the%20attac
k,primary%20source%20of%20malicious%20attack'

36. https://www.akamai.com/glossary/what-is-a-quic-flood-ddos-attack#:~:text=Are%20QUIC%20flood%20attacks%20a,sophisticated%20attacks%20like%20QUIC%20floods.

37. https://www.logixal.co.uk/insights/hackers-vs-heroes-the-real-stories-behind-cybersecurity-wins-and-fails

38. https://dev.to/harperdb/reducing-data-latency-with-geographically-distributed-databases-41oa#:~:text=Many%20organizations%20have%20come%20to%20accept%20cloud,long%20distance%20routing.%20Thus%2C%20latency%20is%20solved!

39. https://www.greatamericaninsurancegroup.com/content-hub/loss-control/details/zero-trust-security-a-modern-approach-to-cybersecurity#:~:text=Core%20Principles%20of%20Zero%20Trust%20Security%20Verify,expectation%20that%20a%20breach%20may%20already%20exist.

40. https://www.atlassian.com/incident-management/incident-response/lifecycle#nist-incident-response-lifecycle

41. https://www.researchgate.net/publication/265294758_A_Review_of_DDOS_Attack_and_its_Countermeasures_in_TCP_Based_Networks

42. https://eventussecurity.com/cybersecurity/resilience/

43. https://www.mimecast.com/blog/botnet-detection-and-removal/

44. https://www.interpol.int/es/Noticias-y-acontecimientos/Noticias/2016/Avalanche-network-dismantled-in-international-cyber-operation#:~:text=Around%2020%20different%20malware%20families,.gov.uk/blog.

45. https://www.europol.europa.eu/media-press/newsroom/news/world%E2%80%99s-most-dangerous-malware-emotet-disrupted-through-global-action#:~:text=27%20Jan%202021,Against%20Criminal%20Threats%20(EMPACT).

46. https://www.scrut.io/post/cybersecurity-governance#:~:text=Core%20principles%20include%20accountability%2C%20transparency,CISA%20play%20in%20cybersecurity%20governance?

47. https://www.ftc.gov/business-guidance/small-businesses/cybersecurity/nist-framework

48. https://insights.pecb.com/iso-iec-27001-and-iso-iec-27035-building-a-resilient-cybersecurity-strategy-for-2024/

49. https://auditboard.com/blog/cobit

50. https://csrc.nist.gov/news/2025/nist-revises-sp-800-61#:~:text=NIST%20Revises%20SP%20800%2D61:%20Incident%20Response%20Recommendations%20and%20Cons

iderations,April%2003%2C%202025&text=Incident%20response%20is%20a%20critical,Computer%20Security%20Incident%20Handling%20Guide.

51. https://www.techtarget.com/searchsecurity/definition/Computer-Fraud-and-Abuse-Act-CFAA#:~:text=Aug%2001%2C%202023-,What%20is%20the%20Computer%20Fraud%20and%20Abuse%20Act%20(CFAA)?,one%20of%20the%20following%20results:

52. https://www.europol.europa.eu/how-we-work/services-support/joint-cybercrime-action-taskforce#:~:text=(J%2DCAT)-,Fighting%20cybercrime%20worldwide,key%20cybercrime%20threats%20and%20targets.

53. https://cybilportal.org/actors/cyber-threat-alliance-cta/#:~:text=The%20Cyber%20Threat%20Alliance%20(CTA,organizations%20in%20the%20cybersecurity%20field.

54. https://medium.com/@d21dcs151/a-case-study-on-mirai-botnet-attack-of-2016-4b66630e6508

55. https://www.sciencedirect.com/science/article/pii/S1084804525000074

56. https://innefu.com/ai-in-defence-how-artificial-intelligence-is-powering-tomorrows-military/#:~:text=1.,5.

57. https://www.sysdig.com/blog/ddos-as-a-service-the-rebirth-botnet